THE BIBLE

REDISCOVERING GOD'S VOICE
IN AN AGE OF CONFUSION

ROBERT GRIFFITH

GRACE AND TRUTH PUBLISHING
P.O. Box 338, Gunnedah NSW 2380 Australia
www.graceandtruthpublishing.com.au

ISBN 978-1-7642635-4-2

A NOTE FROM THE AUTHOR

I did not set out to write another book about the Bible. The world already has shelves full of those books. What compelled me to write this book is a deepening burden. In recent years I have been watching the church drift, often without realising it, from the solid ground of Scripture. Yes, the Bible may still be quoted, studied, and preached from many pulpits, but increasingly it is being twisted, reinterpreted, or used to endorse whatever people already believe. I fear that we are losing the ability to hear what God really said, and to trust the Holy Spirit who still speaks today through the Bible.

It was that burden which birthed what may end up being my most important book. My conviction here is simple: The same Spirit who inspired Scripture must also guide its readers. Without the Spirit, the Bible becomes either a museum piece or a mirror of our own flawed opinions. With Him, it is a living revelation of the heart of God who still calls, corrects, and comforts His people.

I truly believe we are living in one of the most biblically confused generations in church history. We have greater access to Scripture than any believers before us, yet we often handle the Bible with less respect and less understanding. The real tragedy is not that people disagree about what the Bible means, but that so few of us take the time to listen as the Spirit interprets it. We speculate where He has chosen silence and grow silent where He has spoken clearly.

This book is therefore my humble, but very sincere attempt to call us back to confidence in the Bible, not as an idol to defend but as a revelation to embrace; back to dependence on the Holy Spirit, who inspired both the words and also the wisdom of what was left unwritten; back to humility before the our God whose truth sets us all free.

I invite you now to meet again the God we have learned to quote but forgotten to know, as we transition from reading about God to really walking with Him again. This book is a call to rediscover the living heart behind the written word.

Robert Griffith

TABLE OF CONTENTS

INTRODUCTION

The Bible has been called the greatest story ever told, and rightly so. Yet for many, it has also become the most confusing story ever read. Across centuries and cultures, this sacred text has shaped laws, inspired art, comforted the grieving, and sparked multiple movements that changed the world. It has also been twisted to justify violence, oppression, and pride. The same book that has brought life to millions of people has, in careless hands, been used to mislead, wound and even kill. How can this be? How can a book that reveals the heart of God be so easily misunderstood by those who claim to love Him?

That question has troubled me for years. I have spent most of my adult life preaching, teaching, and living under the authority of Scripture. I have seen its power to awaken hearts and transform lives when read with humility and the help of the Holy Spirit.

But I have also seen the confusion and damage that arises when people lift verses out of context, ignore the original intent of the authors, or treat the Bible as a weapon rather than a window into the loving heart of God. The tragedy is not that people disagree about Scripture - that has always been the case - but that so few take the time to really learn how to read the Bible correctly.

As mentioned in my Author's note, this book was birthed from that burden. I wanted to write something that was clear enough for the ordinary believer yet rich enough to satisfy the thoughtful seeker. It is not an academic textbook, though it draws on serious scholarship. Nor is it a devotional book filled with sentimental reflections, though it aims to warm the heart.

My main goal here is to build a bridge between understanding and devotion - to help ordinary believers grasp the extraordinary story of how God has spoken through human words, and how He still speaks through them today. If we can learn to approach the Bible as it was always meant to be approached – which is with reverence, context, and dependence on the Spirit - then its pages will become not a source of confusion but a wellspring of life.

We will begin by exploring what the Bible really is. It is so much more than a religious anthology or moral code; it is the record of God's revelation - His self-disclosure through history, poetry, prophecy, and ultimately through Jesus Christ. Understanding that will change everything. When we say the Bible is *"the Word of God,"* we are not claiming that God dictated words to passive scribes. We are saying that the eternal God has chosen to reveal Himself through human language, personality, experience and culture. That miracle - divine truth expressed through human words - is the starting point of faith.

We will then trace the story of how these words were gathered, preserved, and recognised as Scripture. We will look at why the Bible can always be trusted historically and spiritually, and why it remains unlike any other book. From there, we will consider how to read it correctly - how to respect context, recognise the centrality of Christ, and rely on the Spirit who inspired it. And finally, we will learn how to live under its authority, allowing the Bible not just to inform us but to transform us.

This book does not seek to add to Scripture but to help us hear it again. My deepest longing is that readers will fall in love with the Bible as it reveals the living Word of God - alive, active, and sharper than a double-edged sword.

We live in an age of noise and opinion. Everyone has something to say, but few are listening to the God who still speaks. My hope is that as you turn these pages, you will rediscover that still, small voice - the voice that called creation into being, that thundered on Sinai, that whispered to Elijah, and that took on flesh in Jesus Christ. The Bible is not a relic of the past; it is the living testimony of a God who refuses to be silent.

So let us begin this journey together - not as scholars dissecting an ancient manuscript, but as longing disciples walking on holy ground. May the Spirit who inspired those words so long ago, now illuminate our hearts to understand them fully. And may we once again hear, through ink and paper, the eternal voice of the living God – as the Spirit reveals God's heart on every page.

1. THE WORD BEHIND THE WORDS

Before there were scrolls, before ink touched parchment or letters were carved in stone, there was a Voice. The Bible begins not with a writer's pen, it begins with a divine word: *"And God said, 'Let there be light.'"* (Genesis 1:3). From that very first utterance, creation itself came alive.

God did not build the universe with tools or material; He spoke, and reality obeyed. The story of the Scriptures begins with sound - the living God revealing Himself through words that carry life, power, and purpose.

The Bible is therefore not merely a collection of ancient writings but the record of divine speech - God making Himself known. Long before anyone could hold a Bible in their hands, humanity was already being directly addressed by its Author. Revelation has preceded writing; encounter has preceded explanation. The first listeners were not actually readers at all - they were hearers who responded to a God who spoke into their world.

When we call the Bible *the Word of God*, we are pointing beyond paper and ink to the reality that stands behind them: the eternal, self-revealing God. The Scriptures are His primary means of communication, but they are not the end in themselves. Just as a window is valuable because of the light it lets through, so the Bible is precious because it reveals the living God who speaks through it. We honour the text not as an idol but as a doorway into the divine presence.

This understanding guards us from two equal and opposite errors. One is bibliolatry – which is treating the Bible as an object of worship rather than the means by which we worship God. The other is disregard - treating it as a human artifact, admirable perhaps, but optional.

The truth lies between these extremes: Scripture is fully human in its form yet fully divine in its origin. It bears the fingerprints of its writers while carrying the breath of its Author.

Paul captured this mystery when he wrote in 2 Timothy 3:16, *"All Scripture is God-breathed and is useful for teaching, rebuking, correcting and training in righteousness."* *God-breathed* translates the Greek *theopneustos* - literally *"breathed out by God."* The image is vivid: as a person's breath carries their voice, so the breath of God carries His Word. Inspiration is not dictation but respiration - God breathing His life through human expression.

This miracle of inspiration does not erase human individuality; it actually redeems it. The prophets thundered, the poets wept, the apostles reasoned, and through their distinct voices God spoke one consistent message. Each writer brought personality, vocabulary, and experience, yet all were moved by the same Spirit. Peter describes this process beautifully: *"For prophecy never had its origin in the human will, but prophets, though human, spoke from God as they were carried along by the Holy Spirit."* (2 Peter 1:21)

The phrase *'carried along'* evokes the image of a ship driven by the wind. The sailors hoist their sails and steer, but the wind provides the power. Likewise, the human authors of Scripture hoisted the sails of language and culture, yet it was the breath of God Himself which filled every sail. Inspiration is cooperation without confusion - the divine and the human are working in perfect harmony.

Because of this, Scripture is trustworthy in all it intends to teach. Its authority does not rest on the moral perfection of its writers but on the character of the God who inspired them. When God speaks, His Word carries His own nature: truthful, faithful, and powerful. Isaiah declared, *"So is my word that goes out from my mouth: It will not return to me empty but will accomplish what I desire and achieve the purpose for which I sent it."* (Isaiah 55:11). That promise applies to every page of the Bible.

The authority of the Scriptures therefore flows from the Author Himself. To read the Bible is to stand under the voice of the living God. Yet God's communication is never mechanical; it is always relational. He speaks not to disseminate information but to invite fellowship.

From the very beginning, divine speech has always been the language of relationship. God's words to Adam and Eve in the Garden of Eden were not commands shouted from a distance; they were expressions of love and purpose, guiding humanity into communion with their Creator.

Even after sin fractured that fellowship, God did not remain silent. He called Abraham, instructed Moses, spoke through the prophets, and finally revealed Himself in the person of His Son. *"In the past God spoke to our ancestors through the prophets at many times and in various ways, but in these last days he has spoken to us by his Son."* (Hebrews 1:1–2). The Word of God is not only written; it is incarnate. Jesus Christ is the living Word - the perfect revelation of the invisible God.

This means the written Word must always be read in the light of the living Word. The Scriptures bear witness to Christ; they are never a substitute for Him. When Jesus rebuked the religious scholars of His day, He said, *"You study the Scriptures diligently because you think that in them you have eternal life. These are the very Scriptures that testify about me."* (John 5:39). So the purpose of Scripture is always to lead us to the Saviour, not to replace Him. Whenever we separate the Bible from the person of Christ, we risk turning revelation into religion and truth into theory.

Understanding Scripture as both divine and human also helps us appreciate its variety. It speaks through story, song, prophecy, letter, and vision. The Bible does not flatten human experience into one style; it embraces the full range of human emotion and intellect. We hear the lament of Jeremiah, the poetry of David, the logic of Paul, and the parables of Jesus - and through them all, one consistent divine heartbeat. The diversity of Scripture is clear evidence of its authenticity: God meets humanity where humanity actually lives.

This is why the Bible continues to speak across all cultures and centuries. Its words were shaped in ancient languages, yet they carry timeless truth. When translated faithfully, the same Spirit who inspired the originals continues to illuminate their meaning for every generation.

The power of Scripture does not depend on its age or its style but on the presence of the living God who breathes through it still. To approach such a book requires humility. The Bible is not a puzzle to be solved but a mystery to be entered. When we open its pages, we are not mastering information but being mastered by revelation.

The Psalmist captured this posture perfectly: *"Your word is a lamp for my feet, a light on my path."* (Psalm 119:105). A lamp does not reveal the whole journey at once; it provides just enough light for the next step. In much the same way, God's Word in the Bible guides the humble heart moment by moment, revealing truth as we are ready to walk in it.

Yet humility alone is not enough; dependence is also essential. Without the Holy Spirit, the Bible can become a closed book - a source of arguments rather than transformation. The Spirit who inspired the text must also illuminate the reader. Only then does Scripture accomplish its original divine purpose. Paul prayed that believers would receive *"the Spirit of wisdom and revelation, so that you may know him better."* (Ephesians 1:17). That must remain the prayer of every faithful reader today.

When we read with the Holy Spirit's help, the Bible ceases to be a museum of religious artefacts and becomes a meeting place with God. Its stories breathe again; its commands convict; its promises strengthen. The same power that spoke light into the darkness now speaks life into our souls. Reading the Bible in this way is not an academic exercise but an act of worship.

It is also an act of trust. To believe that these words are inspired is to rest in the faithfulness of the One who gave them. We may not understand every detail or reconcile every mystery, but we can trust that God has revealed enough for faith and obedience. The gaps and tensions in the text are not flaws but invitations - to seek, to listen, to depend. As we do, we discover that behind every word stands the Word Himself, patient and unchanging. The miracle of the Bible is not only that it exists, but that it still speaks to us today.

Empires have risen and fallen, languages have shifted, critics have come and gone, and yet the voice of God continues to echo through its pages. Generations find themselves addressed by words written long before their time yet perfectly suited to their hearts. This endurance is not a human achievement; it is divine preservation.

To encounter the Word behind the words, then, is to encounter God Himself. The same breath that gave life to Adam now breathes through the Scriptures, awakening faith and shaping hearts. As we read, we are drawn into the ongoing conversation between Creator and creation - a dialogue that began in Genesis and will find its final *"Amen"* in Revelation.

So, we begin where all true theology begins: with the God who speaks. He is not distant or silent but near and personal. He desires to be known, and He has chosen to make Himself known through words - words that reveal His nature, His purposes, and His redeeming love. The Bible is the enduring testimony of that revelation, the living record of divine communication. Behind every sentence in the Bible stands the speaking God, inviting us to listen and live.

The voice of God has always carried authority and tenderness. When Scripture speaks, it bears the same tone. The God who thundered from Sinai is also the Shepherd who whispers comfort beside still waters. His Word commands, but it also consoles. Understanding this dual character of divine speech is essential to grasping what the Bible truly is: not a static rulebook, but the living communication of a relational God.

Human speech can only describe reality; divine speech *creates* it. When God speaks, things come into being that did not exist before. The psalmist declared, *"By the word of the Lord the heavens were made, their starry host by the breath of his mouth."* (Psalm 33:6). Every star that burns in the night sky is a testament to that original command. God's Word is not merely information - it is formation. It brings into existence the very world in which His creatures live and move.

That same creative power operates when Scripture is read with faith. The Word that once created worlds now creates faith within the human heart. As Paul wrote, *"Consequently, faith comes from hearing the message, and the message is heard through the word about Christ."* (Romans 10:17). The Bible is not a record of what God *used* to say; it is the medium through which He *still* speaks. Each generation encounters afresh the same living voice.

This means that reading Scripture is never a neutral undertaking. Whenever we open the Bible, something very real happens. We are standing once again before the God who speaks worlds into being. His Word calls, confronts, comforts, and commissions. It exposes motives we did not know we had and reveals hopes we thought were lost. *"For the word of God is alive and active. Sharper than any double-edged sword, it penetrates even to dividing soul and spirit, joints and marrow; it judges the thoughts and attitudes of the heart."* (Hebrews 4:12). The same power that formed galaxies now searches the human soul.

Yet many believers struggle to hear that living voice. For some, the Bible feels silent or remote; for others, it has become overly familiar. The danger of familiarity is that we can then mistake recognition for understanding. We think we know the text just because we have heard it before. But divine words cannot be exhausted by repetition. They always yield new meaning when approached in faith, because the Author is alive.

The Holy Spirit's presence is what distinguishes biblical reading from any other form of reading. Literature can move us, poetry can inspire us, history can instruct us - but only Scripture, when illuminated by the Spirit, can *transform* us. Without Him, even the most careful study remains on the surface. With Him, the same words pierce the heart and renew the mind. The difference lies not in the text but in the reader's openness to the Spirit's illumination. This is why prayer must accompany interpretation. The early church Fathers often prayed before reading Scripture, asking that the veil be lifted from their eyes. Their practice echoes the psalmist's plea: *"Open my eyes that I may see wonderful things in your law."* (Psalm 119:18)

That simple prayer still remains the doorway to all revelation. Intellectual effort matters, but illumination is ultimately a gift. The dynamic between divine inspiration and human reception means that Scripture is simultaneously ancient and immediate. It was completed a long time ago, yet it continues to address new circumstances with startling relevance. When we read, we are not dragging an old text into the present; the eternal Word is reaching from eternity into our moment. The Spirit collapses the distance between then and now so that the same God who spoke to Moses, Isaiah, or Mary, speaks now to us.

Because Scripture is relational, it demands response. God's Word never leaves a listener unchanged. Some resist it; others are remade by it. When Israel first heard the law read aloud, the people wept because they recognised how far they had strayed from God's will. But those tears were not condemnation - they were the beginning of renewal. The Word exposed their need and then offered grace. Nehemiah told them, *"Do not grieve, for the joy of the Lord is your strength."* (Nehemiah 8:10). That is the rhythm of Scripture: revelation followed by redemption.

In our modern age of endless commentary, it is too easy to let second-hand opinions replace direct encounter. We can become students of people's analysis rather than students of Scripture. Commentaries, sermons, and study guides are valuable servants but very poor masters. They help illuminate the text, yet they must never stand between us and the voice of God. The ultimate authority rests not in human explanation but always in divine revelation.

When we approach the Bible, therefore, we do so not to master it but to be mastered by it. We bow before a Word that outranks every philosophy and every fashion. It is this conviction that has sustained the church through persecution and doubt. Believers have clung to the Scriptures not because they were fashionable or simple but because they are true. The Word of God has been chained in prisons, burned in squares, and banned in nations, yet it refuses to die. Like its Author, the Bible always rises again.

The enduring life of Scripture is one of the greatest proofs of its divine origin. Human writings will fade when the culture that produced them has disappeared; God's Word transcends every culture. Empires have rewritten history to suit their power, yet the Bible has survived them all, unchanged in its essential message. It continues to confront kings and comfort the poor, to outlive regimes and outshine philosophies. *"The grass withers and the flowers fall, but the word of our God endures forever."* (Isaiah 40:8)

That endurance is not accidental; it is providential. God guards His Word because His Word guards His people. The same Spirit who inspired the text preserves it down through history. Every translation, every rediscovery, every revival has been the Spirit's way of ensuring that no generation is left without light. Even the difficult seasons - when Scripture was ignored or suppressed - only make its resilience more remarkable. Each time the Word has been buried, it has risen with greater power.

This divine preservation also reminds us that revelation is complete yet inexhaustible. Nothing can be added to the canon of Scripture, for God has said all that is necessary for faith and salvation. Yet what He has said continues to unfold in meaning and application. Like sunlight refracted through different windows, the same truth illuminates every context in new ways. The Bible is not a static monument but a living stream, and the Spirit invites each believer to drink deeply from it.

Because the Word is living, it will speak differently to different hearts. To one person, a verse will bring conviction; to another, comfort. The same passage that once warned now encourages, depending on where we stand in our journey. This adaptability is not inconsistency - it is intimacy. The Author knows His readers. He applies His Word personally, meeting each of us in our need. Jesus promised, *"The Advocate, the Holy Spirit, whom the Father will send in my name, will teach you all things and will remind you of everything I have said to you."* (John 14:26). The Holy Spirit is both Teacher and Reminder, ensuring that God's Word is never a distant echo but a present voice.

This explains why memorising Scripture has always been a vital spiritual discipline. When God's Word is hidden in our hearts, it becomes available to the Spirit at any moment. The psalmist testified, *"I have hidden your word in my heart that I might not sin against you."* (Psalm 119:11). In times of trial, temptation, or confusion, verses once read long ago return to mind with living force. The Spirit draws from the reservoir of Scripture within us, bringing guidance that no external source could provide.

However, the Word cannot dwell richly in us if it is not read. Many Christians confess that they struggle with consistency in reading the Bible, often because they view it as duty rather than delight. The key to joy in Scripture is not quantity but encounter. A single verse read with openness can change a life. The goal is not to rush through chapters but to meet the Author in the text. When that happens, even familiar words ignite with new fire.

The church's task is to nurture this love for the Word. Preaching and teaching are not performances but acts of service to the text. The preacher's authority is derived, not inherent; it flows from faithful exposition of what God has already spoken. Every sermon should echo the humility of the centurion who said, *"But say the word, and my servant will be healed."* (Luke 7:7). The preacher speaks only because God has first spoken.

Likewise, every believer becomes a messenger of the Word. The Bible is not meant to end with us but to flow through us. When Scripture shapes our thinking, our speech begins to carry its cadence; our actions reflect its truth. The early church turned the world upside down not because they possessed scrolls but because those scrolls had possessed *them*. They became living epistles, read by everyone who encountered them. Paul wrote, *"You show that you are a letter from Christ, the result of our ministry, written not with ink but with the Spirit of the living God, not on tablets of stone but on tablets of human hearts."* (2 Corinthians 3:3)

To encounter the Word behind the words is therefore to become a word yourself - a testimony of grace, a reflection of divine truth. The Scriptures do not merely inform us about God; they form Christ within us.

The same Spirit who inspired prophets and apostles now writes on our hearts, turning readers into witnesses. For this reason, the study of Scripture is never an end in itself. Knowledge without obedience hardens the heart; obedience without knowledge can mislead it. The Spirit unites both, giving us understanding so that we may live faithfully. When head and heart meet under the authority of the Word, transformation occurs. Our worldview shifts; our values realign; our lives bear fruit that lasts.

This is what it means to say that the Bible is *"living and active."* It lives because God lives; it acts because God acts. Every time we engage it with faith, it recreates something within us. The same power that spoke light into darkness now speaks holiness into our humanity. The same Spirit who hovered over the waters of creation now hovers over the pages of Scripture, bringing order to the chaos of our souls.

To read the Bible well, then, is to participate in a dynamic divine conversation that began before time. Each page invites us to listen and respond, to echo back praise, worship, confession, and commitment. The written Word leads us to the living Word; the living Word leads us to the Father. The cycle of revelation and response continues until all creation joins the final chorus of worship.

Behind every word of Scripture stands the voice that spoke the universe into being and the cross into history. That voice has not grown weaker with time. It still calls, convicts, and comforts. It still creates faith where there was none. And it still waits for attentive hearts who will listen.

The Bible does not exist merely to be admired but to be obeyed. Divine revelation always beckons a human response. Every page of the Bible carries within it an implicit invitation: *Will you trust Me?* The Bible's authority is not meant to crush the reader but to call the reader into freedom. Jesus said, *"If you hold to my teaching, you are really my disciples. Then you will know the truth, and the truth will set you free."* (John 8:31–32). The freedom promised here is not independence from authority, it is deliverance through obedience.

When we acknowledge Scripture as the voice of God, we place ourselves under its judgment and its grace. We allow its words to test our motives, correct our assumptions, and reorder our desires. The same Word that comforts also confronts. It exposes hypocrisy while offering healing. The prophets understood this tension well: Jeremiah described God's Word as *"a fire... and a hammer that breaks a rock in pieces."* (Jeremiah 23:29). Fire purifies; a hammer shapes. The Word burns away what is false and forms what is true.

This shaping work happens slowly. Reading the Bible once or twice cannot accomplish it. The Spirit uses repeated exposure - daily hearing, pondering, and obeying - to slowly chisel away everything that resists Christ's likeness. The goal is not mere information but transformation, the renewal of the mind that Paul described in Romans 12:2, *"Do not conform to the pattern of this world but be transformed by the renewing of your mind."*

Transformation begins when we treat Scripture as conversation rather than commentary. Every encounter with the Bible is a dialogue between the living God and His people. We speak when we pray; we listen when we read. Silence before the Word is not passivity but participation - it is the stillness that allows the divine voice to penetrate beneath the noise of our opinions. Elijah discovered that God's presence was not in the wind, the earthquake, or the fire, *"but in a gentle whisper."* (1 Kings 19:12). The same whisper meets us today when we open the Bible with listening hearts.

To listen well, we must approach the Bible with both reverence and expectancy. Reverence recognises whose voice we are hearing; expectancy believes that He still has something to say. Reverence without expectancy will lead to ritual; expectancy without reverence leads to presumption. The two together create the posture of true discipleship. When the early believers *"devoted themselves to the apostles' teaching"* (Acts 2:42), they were not attending lectures but receiving life. The Word was shaping a community, not merely instructing individuals.

Communal listening remains vital today. God never intended His Word to be interpreted in isolation. In the gathered church, Scripture is read aloud so that hearts are united around a single authority higher than any human leader. This shared hearing protects us from private distortions and reminds us that the Bible was given to a people, not a collection of spiritual consumers. When the church listens together, truth takes root collectively.

Nevertheless, personal engagement is equally necessary. The corporate reading of Scripture fuels but does not replace the private encounter. Each believer is called to meet God in the quiet place - to wrestle, to question, and to receive. The pattern established by Jesus Himself points the way: *"Very early in the morning, while it was still dark, Jesus got up, left the house and went off to a solitary place, where he prayed."* (Mark 1:35). Prayer and Scripture belong together; they form the rhythm of communion.

In that rhythm we discover that obedience is not a burden but a blessing. The commands of God are not arbitrary rules designed to restrict; they are revelations of reality. To obey them is to live in alignment with truth. The psalmist rejoiced, *"The law of the Lord is perfect, refreshing the soul. The statutes of the Lord are trustworthy, making wise the simple."* (Psalm 19:7). When we submit to the Word, we step into wisdom; when we resist it, we invite confusion.

Modern culture often treats authority as the enemy of freedom. Yet biblical authority is the foundation of true liberty. Only under the reign of truth can the soul be at rest. The person who rejects divine authority does not escape rule; they simply trade a benevolent King for the tyranny of self. The irony is that self-rule always leads to bondage. By contrast, those who bow to God's Word find peace. *"Great peace have those who love your law, and nothing can make them stumble."* (Psalm 119:165)

The authority of Scripture therefore can never be reduced to intellectual assent; it must become embodied obedience. The Word must take flesh again in every generation - first in Christ, now in His people.

The early church was recognised not by its arguments but by its actions. They cared for the poor, honoured the truth, forgave their enemies, and proclaimed Christ crucified because they had heard and believed what God had said. Their lives became living commentaries on the gospel.

This embodiment of the Word remains the calling of every believer. The Bible does not exist to be admired on a shelf or quoted for effect; it is meant to be incarnated. When its truth becomes visible in our behaviour, Scripture finds its fullest expression. We become the evidence that God still speaks. The world reads our lives before it ever reads our Bibles. That is why Paul urged Timothy, *"Preach the word; be prepared in season and out of season; correct, rebuke and encourage - with great patience and careful instruction."* (2 Timothy 4:2). The preacher's task is not to invent truth but to transmit it faithfully until hearers themselves become living testimonies.

Faithful transmission requires courage and humility - courage to speak the Word when it is unpopular, and humility to remain under it while speaking. The greatest danger for those who handle Scripture is to believe they stand above it. We may defend the Bible eloquently yet neglect to let it defend us from pride. The Word is sharper than the preacher; and it cuts both ways. Whenever we proclaim it honestly, it first pierces our own hearts.

Every generation faces the temptation to reshape Scripture to fit its culture. Sometimes the pressure is only subtle, appealing to compassion or modern sensibility; at other times it is overt, demanding silence on uncomfortable truths. But God's Word does not bend to fashion. It judges every age even as it blesses it. When believers hold fast to Scripture amid cultural drift, they become prophetic witnesses - signs of a kingdom not built by human hands. *"Heaven and earth will pass away, but my words will never pass away."* (Matthew 24:35)

This faithfulness, however, must always be marked by love. Truth without love becomes tyranny; love without truth just becomes sentimentality.

The Bible unites both perfectly because its Author is both holy and merciful. The same Word that pronounces judgment also offers grace. The cross itself is the intersection of these realities - the place where divine justice and compassion meet. To live by the Word is to live daily under the shadow of that cross, where obedience and mercy walk hand in hand.

When the Word governs our lives, it reshapes our imagination. We begin to see the world not through cynicism or fear but through promise. Scripture trains us to notice redemption where others see ruin. It reveals that history is not random but ruled by providence. Even the chaos of our modern time is held within the purposes of a speaking God who will have the last word. Revelation assures us that the final voice we hear will not be the noise of rebellion but the declaration from the throne: *"It is done."* (Revelation 21:6)

Until that moment, the church must listen and obey. We live between revelation given and revelation fulfilled, guided by the Scriptures that testify to both. The Bible is the anchor of our hope because it reveals the One who cannot lie. In its pages we meet the same Christ who walked with the disciples on the road to Emmaus and *"explained to them what was said in all the Scriptures concerning himself."* (Luke 24:27). That conversation has never ended; it continues every time we open the Book and recognise His voice.

To recognise His voice is the ultimate aim of reading the Bible. The goal is not mastery of texts but intimacy with the Author. When we hear Him speaking through Scripture, everything changes - our fears, our priorities, our very identity. We discover that the Bible's grand story is not merely about ancient Israel or the early church but about God's relentless, passionate pursuit of relationship with humanity. The Word that called creation into existence is the same Word that calls us by name. Therefore, let the reading of Scripture become an act of worship. Approach the Bible with the reverence of Moses before the burning bush, removing the sandals of self-assurance, aware that the ground upon which you stand is indeed holy.

In those moments of stillness, the printed page becomes sacred space and the ink becomes flame. The voice that once said *"Let there be light"* still speaks light into our darkness.

This is the Word behind the words - the living Christ revealed through the written testimony of His Spirit. To encounter Him is to be changed forever. The pages close, but the conversation continues. For as long as God's people listen, the divine voice will not be silent, and the world will go on being remade by the power of His Word.

It is my prayer that this one chapter alone will have ignited a fire within you to embrace the Bible with a renewed passion and a deep and profound respect and awe as the God who spoke the world into being, now speaks to you. If this introductory chapter has not ignited that fire in you – then perhaps you should lay this book aside for a season and pick it up another day. Without that fire, the rest of what is written here will not achieve its goal.

However, if you do feel a renewed wonder and respect for the greatest book ever written, then what remains here will change your entire approach to the Bible. If you are a preacher or Bible teacher then I believe there is an urgency for you read on, as I am praying that God will completely transform your approach to this ancient text and give you a renewed ability to teach His Word to others and inspire them to embrace God's Word.

But if you are not one who is called to expound the truths of the Bible to others from a platform, you are still called to live those truths in the community in which God has placed you. Spending time working through this book will equip you in ways you never dreamed you needed to be equipped! It will help you answer many questions and open many doors into people's hearts as you allow the Bible to come alive in you and draw people to the One you encounter afresh within its pages.

So, my brother or sister, let us take this journey together, shall we? If reading this book has even half the impact it did on me as I wrote it, then your life is about to change!

2. THE AUTHORITY OF SCRIPTURE

Authority rooted in the nature of God

Every claim of authority must rest on the character of the one who gives it. Human authority will often depend on power, position, or persuasion. Divine authority flows from truth itself. God does not command because He is strong; God commands because He is right. His authority is the natural extension of His holiness and love. To acknowledge God's authority, therefore, is to recognise His goodness and wisdom, not merely His might.

The Bible's authority begins here. Scripture is not authoritative because a church declared it so or because it has survived for centuries. It carries authority because it bears witness to the self-revealing God whose very being is truth.

When God speaks, His words are binding - not because they are forced upon us but because reality itself bends to His will. *"For the word of the Lord is right and true; He is faithful in all He does."* (Psalm 33:4). The authority of Scripture is the authority of the God it reveals.

Revelation and response

God's revelation is never just a monologue. He speaks to invite relationship. Authority, in biblical terms, is not domination but participation in His truth. From Genesis onward, God's words create, define, and invite. He spoke the world into being, then spoke to humanity so that creation might then live under His guidance. The tragedy of sin is the refusal of divine authority - humans choosing to define good and evil for themselves. Ever since, the Spirit's work has been to re-establish the rule of God's truth in human hearts.

Scripture functions as the written witness to that revelation. It records the unfolding story of God's dealings with His people, climaxing in the revelation of Jesus Christ. Because it is God's chosen instrument for revealing Himself, the Bible carries His authority. To submit to Scripture is to submit to the living God who speaks through it.

Which is why Paul wrote in 2 Timothy 3:16–17,*"All Scripture is God-breathed and is useful for teaching, rebuking, correcting and training in righteousness, so that the servant of God may be thoroughly equipped for every good work."*

Paul's phrase *"God-breathed"* captures the whole mystery: the same divine breath that gave life to Adam now gives life to these words. Yet they remain human - formed by the vocabulary, culture, and emotion of real people. Divine authority does not erase humanity; it elevates it. Through the Spirit, God's truth takes human shape so that we may receive it and respond in faith.

Authority expressed through the Spirit's inspiration

The authority of Scripture cannot be separated from the Holy Spirit. He is not a distant editor ensuring theological accuracy; He is the living presence of God communicating His will through human language. *"For prophecy never had its origin in the human will, but prophets, though human, spoke from God as they were carried along by the Holy Spirit."*(2 Peter 1:21). The phrase *"carried along"* suggests the wind filling the sails of a ship - divine breath moving human vessels toward God's purpose.

This means authority lies not in the personalities of the writers nor in the materials they used but in the Spirit who guided them. What they wrote, God intended. What they did not write, He withheld. Inspiration is thus the Spirit's active governance of truth through human participation. To resist the authority of Scripture, is to resist the Holy Spirit Himself.

Because the Spirit remains present, that authority is not frozen in history. He who inspired the text continues to illuminate that text. Every time we read it, He re-enacts revelation, applying eternal truth to contemporary hearts. The Bible is not a static archive but a living conversation between the Holy Spirit and the people of God. So, authority is both given and experienced – it is firmly established once for all, yet it is also freshly realised whenever believers listen and obey.

The Witness of Jesus to Scripture's Authority

Jesus' own relationship with Scripture anchors Christian confidence in its authority. He quoted it in temptation (*Matthew 4:1–11*), taught it as fulfilled in Himself (*Luke 4:21*), and used it to correct misunderstanding (*Matthew 22:29*). For Him, the written Word was the trustworthy revelation of the Father's will. *"Scripture cannot be set aside,"* He declared (*John 10:35*).

Yet Jesus also demonstrated that true authority lies not in legalistic citation but in the Spirit-given meaning behind the text. He exposed the Pharisees for honouring Scripture with their lips while ignoring its heart. In Him, the letter yielded to the life it pointed toward.

Here lies the model for our submission to biblical authority. We honour Scripture not by weaponising it but by allowing it to lead us to Christ. Authority is fulfilled, not diminished, when the Word becomes flesh in us. The Spirit who inspired the prophets now conforms us to the living Word, so that obedience becomes communion rather than coercion.

Authority confirmed by the Spirit in believers

No external institution can impose the Bible's authority on the human heart. The same Spirit who inspired the text must open our eyes to recognise it. *"The person without the Spirit does not accept the things that come from the Spirit of God but considers them foolishness."* (1 Corinthians 2:14). Authority is always discerned spiritually, not mechanically. This inner witness does not make us judges of Scripture; it makes us its willing subjects. The Spirit confirms its truth, compelling us to trust and obey.

Throughout church history, this has been called the *testimonium Spiritus Sancti* - the testimony of the Holy Spirit. It means the Bible authenticates itself through the Spirit's illumination. The authority of Scripture is therefore self-evident to the believer, not because of blind faith but because the Holy Spirit grants us understanding. When we read with humble hearts, we find the same voice that spoke through the prophets speaking still.

Authority experienced in obedience

The measure of biblical authority is not how loudly we defend it but how deeply we live it. Scripture's authority is vindicated when its truth transforms conduct, restores relationships, and renews hope. Jesus concluded the Sermon on the Mount with the image of two builders: one who heard His words and obeyed, and one who heard and ignored. *"Everyone who hears these words of mine and puts them into practice is like a wise man who built his house on the rock."* (Matthew 7:24). The authority of His teaching was proved in stability during the storm.

So it is with all Scripture. Its authority is not a theory to debate but a reality to inhabit. The Holy Spirit presses its truth into our conscience until obedience becomes joy. When believers align their lives with revealed truth, the world sees that the Bible's authority is not oppressive but liberating - the rule of love that sets people free from the tyranny of self.

Living under God's authority today

Our modern culture often equates authority with control and therefore resists it. Yet divine authority is different. It is the loving wisdom of the Creator guiding His creatures into fullness of life. When Scripture speaks, it does so not to restrict but to restore. It confronts our distortions so that grace may heal them. Submitting to Scripture, then, is not intellectual surrender but spiritual alignment.

The Spirit continues to write the fruit of that authority on human hearts. The prophet Jeremiah foresaw this when he spoke of the new covenant: *"I will put my law in their minds and write it on their hearts. I will be their God, and they will be my people."*(Jer. 31:33). The authority of Scripture is therefore fulfilled when its truth becomes internalised - when the Spirit who once breathed words on parchment now breathes holiness into people.

To live under the authority of Scripture is therefore to live in companionship with the Spirit. We read, listen, and obey, trusting that His truth still speaks.

The authority of Scripture is not an external pressure but an internal presence - the Spirit of God bearing witness to the truth of God in the people of God.

Authority and freedom

For many people, authority and freedom seem like opposites. We fear that to submit to divine authority means we are losing ourselves, surrendering our capacity to think or choose. But biblical authority is the very thing that enables freedom. It is not the imprisonment of the soul but its protection. A fish is not free when it leaves the water; it dies. Freedom is found within the boundaries of design. So it is with us. God's truth defines the environment in which human life can truly flourish.

Jesus declared, *"If you hold to my teaching, you are really my disciples. Then you will know the truth, and the truth will set you free."* (John 8:31-32). Freedom flows from fidelity, not rebellion. To live under the authority of Scripture is to live within the truth that liberates. When the Spirit writes that truth upon the heart, obedience ceases to be external conformity and becomes joyful participation in God's will.

The more we trust Scripture's authority, the freer we become from the tyranny of opinion, culture, and emotion. The Spirit uses the Word to anchor us in the reality of God's unchanging character. Without that anchor, we drift. But under authority, we discover stability, peace, and purpose. True freedom is not the absence of restraint; it is the presence of righteousness.

The Spirit's authority in the church

The authority of Scripture is not only personal but communal. God did not give His Word merely to individuals in isolation but to a people formed by covenant. When the church gathers around Scripture, the Spirit exercises authority through shared listening. Paul reminded Timothy that *"All Scripture is God-breathed and is useful … so that the servant of God may be thoroughly equipped for every good work."* (2 Timothy 3:16-17). The *"servant of God"* in context includes the whole body of believers engaged in ministry together.

Authority expressed through Scripture is therefore relational. No single believer possesses the final word on interpretation. The Spirit distributes insight throughout the community so that truth may be discerned corporately. This guards against pride and error. When the Word is read, preached, and practised within the fellowship of the church, the Spirit unites diverse minds under one Lord.

Throughout history, renewal has come whenever God's people returned to this shared submission. The Reformation cry *sola Scriptura* was not an invitation to private interpretation but a summons to place the entire church once again under the Spirit's voice in Scripture. The Spirit who inspired the text also inhabits the community that hears it. When we yield together, the same power that birthed the early church revives us still.

Authority tested in a fragmented world

We now live in an age of competing authorities - science, politics, celebrity, ideology. Each claims to tell us who we are and how we should therefore live. Amid that noise, Scripture speaks with a different kind of power: quiet, steady, Spirit-breathed truth. Its authority does not shout; it stands. *"The grass withers and the flowers fall, but the word of our God endures forever."*(Isaiah 40:8). Every human claim will eventually fade away; only divine truth remains.

Because Scripture's authority endures, it will always confront the idols of every generation. Sometimes the church itself must be called back under its rule. Whenever we twist Scripture to serve our agendas, we repeat the serpent's ancient question: *"Did God really say..?"* (Genesis 3:1). The Spirit's authority exposes such distortions and restores humility. The Bible is not ours to master; it is God's instrument to master us.

In this fragmented modern age, we need the unifying centre that Scripture provides. Under its authority, diversity finds direction without demanding uniformity. The Spirit speaks the same truth in many tongues, drawing the global church into one obedience.

Wherever believers submit to the voice of Scripture, they find common ground so much deeper than culture or denomination. Authority becomes not a boundary that divides but a foundation that holds.

The Spirit's ongoing witness

The authority of Scripture endures because the Spirit has never ceased to bear witness to it. Jesus promised His disciples, *"When he, the Spirit of truth, comes, he will guide you into all the truth."* (John 16:13). That promise was not confined to the first century. The same Spirit who guided the apostles now guides readers in every generation. He does not add new revelation to Scripture but continually illuminates what has been given, bringing it to life in fresh situations.

This ongoing witness preserves both stability and vitality. Without the Spirit, Scripture would become a museum exhibit – accurate, but lifeless. Without Scripture, spiritual experience would drift into imagination. Together they form a strong, living partnership: the Spirit interprets what He originally inspired, ensuring that authority remains alive and relational. When the Spirit whispers through ancient words, the distance between then and now collapses. God still speaks, and His people still recognise His voice.

Many believers can recall moments when a familiar passage suddenly burned with new meaning, addressing a present need. That is not psychological coincidence; it is divine continuity. The Spirit personalises the authority of Scripture, translating timeless truth into timely guidance. Thus, the Bible is never out-of-date. Its Author is eternally contemporary.

Authority that transforms

The final measure of authority is transformation. Scripture's authority is vindicated not merely in creeds but in character. James wrote, *"Do not merely listen to the word, and so deceive yourselves. Do what it says."* (James 1:22). The Spirit who inspired Scripture now reproduces its truth within us, shaping Christ-like lives.

Every act of forgiveness, every renunciation of pride, every step of faith bears witness that the authority of Scripture is very real. Authority transforms when we let the Holy Spirit move beyond information to formation. The Pharisees could quote the text but missed its heart. The early disciples, filled with the Spirit, lived the text until the world around them noticed. When believers embody the Bible's message, the written Word becomes the living testimony of grace. That is the goal of divine authority - to make us participants in the life it proclaims.

Obedience, then, is not fearful compliance but Spirit-empowered harmony with God's will. As Paul wrote in Philippians 2:13, *"It is God who works in you to will and to act in order to fulfil his good purpose."* The same Spirit who once breathed out Scripture now breathes that will into us. Under authority we find renewal, purpose, and joy.

A bridge toward the story of the Bible

The authority of Scripture cannot be understood apart from the One who gave it, the Spirit who preserves it, and the people who live under it. Yet the question naturally follows: How did this authority come to us in written form? How did the Spirit's voice, first spoken through the prophets and the apostles, become the collection of sacred writings which we now call the Bible? Those questions lead us from theology into history, from principle into process.

Having explored why Scripture carries divine authority, we now turn to the remarkable story of how that authority was expressed through human hands. The same Spirit who inspires faith also shaped the Scriptures themselves. To understand the Bible's authority fully, we must see how the Spirit worked in its making - how revelation became writing, how inspiration guided preservation, and how God ensured that what He wanted said would be said. That is the journey before us.

3. THE MAKING OF THE BIBLE

Remembered revelation

Before a single scroll was written, God's words lived on human lips. The earliest chapters of Genesis describe not authors sitting at desks but storytellers who were passing on revelation. Adam's descendants spoke of the Creator who walked with them in the garden. Noah's family carried the memory of both judgment and mercy through the flood. Abraham, Isaac, and Jacob repeated the promises of a mighty covenant-making God around campfires and altars. Faith was transmitted orally a very long time before it was preserved in ink.

In the ancient Near East, the spoken word also carried immense authority. A person's word was binding; an oath once uttered could not be revoked. How much more so the Word of the living God! When He spoke, His utterance shaped history. *"God is not human, that he should lie, not a human being, that he should change his mind. Does he speak and then not act? Does he promise and not fulfil?"* (Numbers 23:19). Every generation of believers learned that the reliability of their faith rested not on clay tablets but on the character of the One speaking.

God's revelation therefore began as remembered conversation. Parents taught their children what their God had done; elders rehearsed His mighty deeds. The oral transmission of truth was sacred stewardship. To forget God's words was to lose identity itself.

Hence the repeated charge to Israel: *"Only be careful, and watch yourselves closely so that you do not forget the things your eyes have seen or let them fade from your heart as long as you live."* (Deuteronomy 4:9).

Memory became the first sanctuary of Scripture. In time, what had been remembered by faith would also be recorded by hand, as the Spirit moved His servants to preserve revelation for generations to come.

A miracle in human history

The Bible did not descend from heaven bound in leather, nor was it dictated to a single writer in one moment of inspiration. It emerged over more than fifteen centuries, written by dozens of authors in three languages across vastly different cultures and continents. And yet, through all that diversity, it tells one unified story: God's relentless pursuit of relationship with humanity. No other collection of writings in all human history compares to this miracle of coherence.

From shepherds to kings, from prophets to fishermen and poets to physicians, the human contributors to Scripture came from every walk of life. Some wrote from palaces, others from prisons; some in prosperity, others in exile. What binds them together is not education or background but inspiration - the breath of God working through human vessels to reveal His heart. This divine-human partnership is what makes the Bible both accessible and transcendent, simultaneously ancient and timeless.

The making of the Bible, then, is not simply a historical process but a theological testimony. It shows how God uses ordinary means to accomplish extraordinary ends. *"We have this treasure in jars of clay to show that this all-surpassing power is from God and not from us."* (2 Corinthians 4:7). Every stage of Scripture's formation demonstrates that pattern: divine power working through human weakness to preserve perfect truth.

The Old Testament: foundations of faith

The earliest books of the Old Testament record God's revelation to Israel - the detailed story of covenant, law, and promise. The Pentateuch (the first five books of our Bible), traditionally attributed to Moses, provided Israel's constitution and theology. It explained who God is, who His people are, and what it means to live in relationship with Him. The historical books traced the unfolding of that covenant through conquest, the monarchy, rebellion, and exile. The prophets, in turn, interpreted those events, calling the nation back to faithfulness.

Each genre within the Old Testament - law, history, poetry, prophecy - reveals a different facet of divine revelation. Together they form the bedrock of biblical theology. When Jesus and the apostles quoted *"the Scriptures,"* these were the writings they revered. The Old Testament was their only Bible, and every line pointed toward its fulfilment in Christ. As He said, *"Everything must be fulfilled that is written about me in the Law of Moses, the Prophets and the Psalms."* (Luke 24:44)

The formation of the Hebrew canon

The Hebrew Bible did not appear all at once but was gradually recognised through centuries of worship and reflection. The Torah, containing the five books of Moses, was accepted first as the foundation of Israel's faith. Later, the prophetic writings and historical records were added, followed by the poetic and wisdom books.

Jewish tradition eventually grouped these into three sections: the Law (*Torah*), the Prophets (*Nevi'im*), and the Writings (*Ketuvim*). Together they form what Jesus called *"the Law and the Prophets,"* encompassing the entirety of Scripture known to His generation.

The process of recognition was guided by clear spiritual criteria. A book had to be authored by a recognised prophet or under prophetic authority, align with the truth already revealed, and be used consistently in worship. This was not about human approval but spiritual resonance. God's people knew His voice. When they heard it in a text, they responded with reverence. As Jesus said, *"My sheep listen to my voice; I know them, and they follow me."* (John 10:27)

The role of the Scribes

As the Hebrew Scriptures grew, so did the responsibility of preserving them. The scribes became custodians of revelation, copying texts with painstaking accuracy. Their reverence for the divine name alone was extraordinary: before writing *church*, they would lay down their pen, wash their hands, and write the sacred name with a new quill. Such devotion ensured that the transmission of Scripture was an act of worship as much as scholarship.

Centuries later, the Masoretes - Jewish scholars active between the sixth and tenth centuries AD - developed a meticulous system of vowel markings and marginal notes to safeguard pronunciation and meaning. They counted letters, tracked word frequencies, and devised elaborate checksums for every scroll. Their diligence was vindicated spectacularly with the discovery of the Dead Sea Scrolls in 1947, which revealed that the biblical manuscripts copied over a thousand years apart were virtually identical. The God who spoke also preserved what He said.

The Old Testament in the life of Israel

For ancient Israel, Scripture was not a library to be studied but a covenant to be lived. The reading of the Law was woven into the nation's rhythms of worship. During the great feasts, the people would gather to hear the words of Moses proclaimed afresh.

This communal reading was more than tradition; it was renewal. *"Assemble the people - men, women and children, and the foreigners residing in your towns - so they can listen and learn to fear the Lord your God and follow carefully all the words of this law."* (Deuteronomy 31:12). Hearing Scripture reminded Israel who they were. Each generation rediscovered the story of deliverance from Egypt, the covenant at Sinai, and the promises of restoration. Even in exile, the prophets reminded them that God's Word had not failed. Daniel's prayers, Ezra's reforms, and Nehemiah's rebuilding all flowed from confidence in the enduring authority of Scripture. The Law and the Prophets were the nation's lifeline - a record of what God had done and a pledge of what He would yet do.

When the exiles returned to Jerusalem and the temple was rebuilt, Ezra's public reading of the Torah became a defining moment of renewal. The people wept as they listened, overwhelmed by conviction and hope. *"They read from the Book of the Law of God, making it clear and giving the meaning so that the people understood what was being read."* (Nehemiah 8:8). That verse remains one of the clearest biblical statements about the task of interpretation. Scripture was not to be mumbled in mystery but explained for understanding, ensuring that obedience flowed from clarity.

The Old Testament completed

By the time of Jesus, the shape of the Hebrew canon was largely settled. The Law, Prophets, and Writings were recognised as the authoritative Word of God. Other Jewish literature, such as the Wisdom of Solomon or the Maccabean histories, was respected but not considered equal to Scripture. These later writings - often called the *Apocrypha* - provide valuable historical insight but were never regarded by Israel or Jesus as divinely inspired. When the early church inherited the Hebrew Scriptures, it inherited that same conviction.

The final prophet of the Old Testament, Malachi, closed the era of direct revelation with a promise: *"See, I will send the prophet Elijah to you before that great and dreadful day of the Lord comes."* (Malachi 4:5). Then came four centuries of prophetic silence - no new Scripture, but not abandonment either. God was preparing the next act of redemption.

When John the Baptist appeared, his voice shattered the long quiet with the cry, *"Prepare the way for the Lord."* (Matthew 3:3). The Old Covenant had spoken; the New was about to begin.

The unity of the two Testaments

The making of the Bible cannot be understood apart from this divine continuity. The same God who spoke through Moses spoke again through Christ. The covenant given at Sinai was fulfilled at Calvary. The Old Testament is promise; the New is fulfilment. Together they form one revelation, one narrative, one Word. Augustine captured it perfectly: *"The New is in the Old concealed; the Old is in the New revealed."*

Recognising this unity protects us from two extremes. One is to treat the Old Testament as obsolete, forgetting that Jesus and the apostles built their entire message upon it. The other is to read the Old without the light of the New, missing the Christ who stands at its centre. The Bible's making is therefore not merely historical but Christological - it is the unfolding of divine revelation culminating in the incarnate Word. Every book, from Genesis to Revelation, finds its coherence in Him.

The story of the Old Testament's formation is a story of divine faithfulness across generations. From oral tradition to written text, from scroll to canon, God ensured that His revelation would not be lost. The next chapter in that story - the birth of the New Testament - will show how that same Spirit guided the apostles to complete the written testimony of redemption and how the early church recognised the voice of God speaking once more.

The birth of the New Testament

The story of the New Testament begins not with pen and parchment, but with the living Christ. Everything that was eventually written first happened in history. The Gospels, Acts, the letters, and Revelation are all responses to the Word made flesh. The disciples heard, saw, and touched the very presence of God among them.

When John opened his first epistle, he firmly grounded his authority in experience, not imagination: *"That which was from the beginning, which we have heard, which we have seen with our eyes, which we have looked at and our hands have touched - this we proclaim concerning the Word of life."* (1 John 1:1)

In the decades after the resurrection, the gospel spread rapidly across the Roman world. The apostles preached before they wrote. Their first concern was proclamation, not preservation, because they expected Christ's return soon.

But as the years passed, and as eyewitnesses began to die, the need for written testimony became clear. The Spirit who once inspired spoken preaching now inspired written witness. The voice of Christ that had once echoed in marketplaces and synagogues was now being captured on scrolls, ensuring that no generation would be left without His message.

The earliest New Testament writings were the letters of Paul. They were not essays in theology but pastoral correspondence - living documents addressing real people in real places. Yet through them, God revealed timeless truths about grace, faith, and the new covenant.

Paul's words carried divine authority because they came from one personally commissioned by the risen Christ. His letters were circulated among the churches and soon read alongside the Old Testament Scriptures. *"After this letter has been read to you, see that it is also read in the church of the Laodiceans."*(Colossians 4:16). Already the new revelation was being shared as Scripture.

The gospels take shape

As eyewitnesses aged and the church spread further from Jerusalem, the need arose to record the story of Jesus in writing. Each Gospel writer approached that task uniquely, guided by the Spirit to meet different audiences and purposes. Matthew, writing primarily for Jews, emphasised fulfilment of prophecy;

Mark, with brisk urgency, captured the power of Jesus' actions; Luke, the very careful historian, highlighted compassion and inclusion; and John, writing last, drew the theological threads together, revealing the eternal Word behind the human Jesus.

Luke's introduction explains the method and motivation: *"Many have undertaken to draw up an account of the things that have been fulfilled among us… therefore, since I myself have carefully investigated everything from the beginning, I too decided to write an orderly account for you, most excellent Theophilus."* (Luke 1:1–3)

This is not detached history - it is divinely guided testimony written so that readers might believe. As John concluded his Gospel: *"These are written that you may believe that Jesus is the Messiah, the Son of God, and that by believing you may have life in his name."* (John 20:31)

The harmony of four distinct Gospels is itself a witness to divine orchestration. They differ in detail and tone but agree in substance and purpose. No single narrative could contain the fullness of the incarnate Word, so the Spirit raised four voices to testify.

Together they give us a composite portrait - human, divine, historical, and eternal. The Word who became flesh is now preserved in words that bring life.

Acts and the Apostolic church

The book of Acts continues the story where the Gospels leave off. Luke's second volume is the bridge between the ministry of Christ and the mission of the church. It shows how the risen Lord continues His work through the Holy Spirit in His people. Every page of Acts demonstrates that the Word did not stop speaking when Jesus Christ ascended; it began multiplying through His growing number of followers. *"The word of God continued to spread and flourish."* (Acts 12:24)

Acts also provides historical context for Paul's letters and the growth of the early church. It records the Council of Jerusalem, where the apostles, under the Spirit's guidance, affirmed the gospel of grace for all nations. The same principle of discernment that once shaped the Old Testament canon was now shaping the church's understanding of the new revelation. Scripture was being written even as the church learned to live by it.

Letters of faith and formation

The New Testament letters reveal the heartbeat of the early church. They were written to communities learning how to live out the gospel in a world hostile to their faith. Some letters, like Romans, articulate deep theology; others, like Philemon, embody forgiveness in practical relationships.

Together they show that doctrine and discipleship cannot be separated. The Word of God forms both belief and behaviour. These letters were quickly treasured and copied. churches exchanged them just as Paul had instructed, and collections began to circulate.

Within decades, most of the New Testament writings were being read in worship alongside the Hebrew Scriptures. Peter even acknowledges the authority of Paul's writings: *"Our dear brother Paul also wrote to you with the wisdom that God gave him… His letters contain some things that are hard to understand, which ignorant and unstable people distort, as they do the other Scriptures, to their own destruction."* (2 Peter 3:15–16)

By the close of the first century, the church already recognised that God was speaking again through the pen of His apostles.

These letters do more than instruct; they incarnate the gospel. Paul's passion, Peter's humility, John's tenderness, James's practicality - all display the Spirit's work in human personality. Inspiration did not erase individuality; it sanctified it. Through their different voices, one divine message resounds: Christ is Lord, and His Word endures forever.

The revelation of Jesus Christ

The New Testament closes not with a letter of advice but a vision of triumph. John's Revelation gathers every thread of Scripture - law, prophecy, gospel, and promise - into a single tapestry of hope. Written during exile on Patmos, it reminds the church that even persecution cannot silence God's Word. *"Write, therefore, what you have seen, what is now and what will take place later."* (Revelation 1:19) The same command that once came to the prophets now comes to the last apostle: *Write.*

Revelation completes the canon not merely by chronology but by theology. It reveals the final act of redemption when the Word made flesh becomes the reigning King. The story that began, *"Let there be light."* Ends with, *"They will see his face."* (Revelation 22:4) Between those sentences lies the entire history of salvation.

The canon closes with a benediction that seals the written Word for all time: *"I warn everyone who hears the words of the prophecy of this scroll: If anyone adds anything to them, God will add to that person the plagues described in this scroll."* (Revelation 22:18) The voice that once spoke creation into being has spoken finally and fully in Christ.

The completion of the Bible

By the early second century, nearly every church accepted the four Gospels, Acts, Paul's letters, and several general epistles as Scripture. Gradually, the smaller letters and Revelation joined the collection through careful discernment.

The process was organic, guided by the Spirit rather than human decree. Councils in later centuries confirmed what had long been true: God's Word had spoken, and the church had heard.

The Bible is thus not a monument to human achievement but a testimony to divine faithfulness. The same God who inspired prophets and apostles also oversaw the recognition and the preservation of their writings. The making of the Bible reveals the nature of God Himself - consistent, truthful, patient, and sovereign over history. Every manuscript, every translation, every reading congregation stands as proof that He keeps His promises.

The Word that began as a divine voice in the beginning became a written testimony in human history, and it will endure until history's end. The next part of this journey will explore how that inspired record has been preserved, transmitted, and trusted through the centuries so that the same voice can still be heard.

The Word preserved through the ages

Once the final form of the Bible was recognised, the challenge became preservation. The early church faced persecution, poverty, and dispersion, yet the Scriptures survived every attempt to silence them. Roman emperors ordered copies of the sacred texts destroyed, but believers risked their lives to protect and copy them.

When the emperor Diocletian launched his campaign against Christians in AD 303, he decreed that every manuscript be burned. Within a decade, Constantine would commission fifty new copies for the churches of his empire. The Word of God outlived the empire that sought to erase it.

Behind this endurance lay both divine providence and human devotion. The scribes of the early church were spiritual descendants of Israel's copyists - men and women who understood that preserving the Word was itself an act of faith. In candle-lit rooms, they traced each letter with care, knowing that they handled something eternal.

Each generation passed on what it had received, fulfilling the apostolic command: *"What you heard from me, keep as the pattern of sound teaching, with faith and love in Christ Jesus. Guard the good deposit that was entrusted to you."* (2 Timothy 1:13–14)

From scrolls to codices

An important development in this process was the transition from scrolls to codices - bound books resembling the modern form of Scripture. Christians adopted this innovation earlier and more eagerly than other groups, possibly because it allowed the entire New Testament to be kept together in one volume. The codex made the Bible portable, durable, and easy to copy. In a profound sense, it mirrored the faith which it carried: flexible, enduring, and ready to travel.

Early manuscripts like *Codex Sinaiticus* and *Codex Vaticanus* - both from the fourth century - contain nearly the entire Bible. Their beauty lies not only in their craftsmanship but in what they represent: a faith so rooted in the Word that believers invested immense labour and expense to preserve it. These manuscripts, discovered many centuries later, confirm that the Scriptures we read today are substantially the same as those read by the earliest Christians. The hand of providence is visible in the ink of history.

Translation and transmission

As the gospel spread, so did the need for translation. Greek gave way to Latin in the West, Coptic in Egypt, Syriac in the East. Each translation represented both a challenge and a triumph - the challenge of conveying divine truth in new tongues, and the triumph of hearing God's voice in the language of the people. The Word of God does not belong to one culture or dialect; it is as multilingual as creation itself.

The most influential of these early translations was undoubtedly the Latin *Vulgate*, produced by Jerome in the fourth century. Working from Hebrew and Greek texts, Jerome sought accuracy over elegance. His labour shaped Western Christianity for a thousand years.

Though later reformers would return to the original languages for fresh translation, they owed an immense debt to Jerome's devotion. The *Vulgate* preserved Scripture's continuity when much of Europe was illiterate. God ensured that His Word remained audible even when the world's lights dimmed.

The chain of faithful witnesses

Throughout the Middle Ages, the preservation of the Scriptures continued through monks, scholars, and missionaries who believed the Word was worth every cost. In remote monasteries, copyists illuminated pages with gold and lapis, blending beauty and reverence. Each stroke of the quill was an act of worship. Their quiet work laid the foundation for later revival. Without their diligence, there would have been no manuscripts for reformers to translate, no text for printers to publish.

Yet even amid devotion, darkness threatened. The Scriptures were often locked away in Latin, inaccessible to ordinary believers. But God never allows His Word to remain imprisoned for long. In every generation He raises up voices to set it free.

From the Celtic missionaries who carried the gospel to wild northern shores to the scholars who preserved learning through centuries of war, the same divine purpose prevailed: *"The word of the Lord endures forever."* (1 Peter 1:25)

The Word unchained

The invention of the printing press in the fifteenth century transformed the preservation of Scripture into proliferation. What had been the work of lifetimes could now be accomplished in days. When Johannes Gutenberg produced his first major printed work - the Bible - it marked not only a technological revolution but a theological one.

The Word of God could now reach every home, every heart, without dependence on scribes or scholars. For the first time in history, the divine voice could echo simultaneously across continents.

This was not mere progress but providence. The same God who inspired prophets and apostles now inspired inventors and printers. The Reformation that soon followed was fuelled by this access.

Luther's German Bible, Tyndale's English New Testament, and countless other translations turned private reading into a public movement. People who had never heard Scripture in their own tongue suddenly encountered the living Word, and whole societies were transformed. *"The unfolding of your words gives light; it gives understanding to the simple."* (Psalm 119:130)

The reliability of the text

Modern critics have often questioned whether the Bible we possess today is the same as the one originally written. Yet the evidence overwhelmingly supports its integrity. More than five thousand Greek manuscripts of the New Testament exist, some dating within decades of the originals - an astonishing fact unmatched by any other ancient text. When compared, these manuscripts reveal minor variations but remarkable consistency. The message remains unchanged.

Archaeological discoveries have strengthened confidence. The Dead Sea Scrolls, unearthed in the mid-twentieth century, contained copies of the Old Testament which are a thousand years older than previously known manuscripts. When scholars compared them with later versions, they found virtually no significant difference. The preservation of Scripture across millennia testifies to divine oversight. The God who spoke through history has preserved His words within it.

The Bible in the modern world

Today the Bible stands as the most translated, printed, and read book in human history. From papyrus to pixels, it has crossed every barrier of time, language, and culture. Yet its purpose has never changed: to reveal the living God and call His people into fellowship with Him. Technology has multiplied its reach, but the miracle remains the same - hearts transformed by hearing His Word.

"Faith comes from hearing the message, and the message is heard through the word about Christ." (Romans 10:17). Amid such abundance, however, the church faces a new challenge: not access but attention. The Bible competes with countless voices clamouring for authority. The danger is not that the Word will disappear, but that it will be drowned out by noise. The task of believers is therefore not only to distribute Scripture but to model devotion to it—to read, interpret, and live it faithfully so that its authority remains visible in a sceptical world.

The miracle of preservation

The making of the Bible is a miracle written in ink and blood. From the first words spoken in Eden to the final vision on Patmos, the same Spirit has preserved, protected, and proclaimed God's truth through fragile human hands. Empires have fallen, languages have died, cultures have changed, but the Word of God stands unchanged. It has outlived its critics, converted its persecutors, and comforted its martyrs. Its endurance is not proof of our human genius but of divine faithfulness. "Your word, Lord, is eternal; it stands firm in the heavens." (Psalm 119:89)

The Bible's journey - from divine speech to written revelation, from parchment to print, from guarded treasure to global message - reveals the unbroken commitment of God to be known. The same voice that spoke at creation still speaks through its pages. Those who read it with faith join a chorus of witnesses stretching across centuries.

The making of the Bible is, ultimately, the making of a people shaped by that Word - living letters of grace written not with ink but with the Spirit of the living God.

4. THE POWER AND PURPOSE OF SCRIPTURE

The Word that works

The Bible is not a passive document, nor a mere record of ancient wisdom. It is the living instrument of God's will in the world. In 2 Timothy 3:16–17, the apostle Paul captures this truth with clarity and conviction: *"All Scripture is God-breathed and is useful for teaching, rebuking, correcting and training in righteousness, so that the servant of God may be thoroughly equipped for every good work."* This declaration reveals both the power and the purpose of Scripture - its divine origin and its practical intention.

Scripture does not simply inform; it transforms. When the Word of God is read in faith, it accomplishes something. Isaiah records God's own promise: *"So is my word that goes out from my mouth: It will not return to me empty but will accomplish what I desire and achieve the purpose for which I sent it."* (Isaiah 55:11). The Bible is not a static collection of sayings but a dynamic channel through which the living God continues to act. His Word does not return void because it carries His breath - the same breath that once spoke creation into being.

This is why the Scriptures will endure. Empires fall, languages change, philosophies fade, yet the Word of God continues to do its work. Every generation rediscovers its power because every generation stands in need of its truth. The Bible does not merely describe the work of God; it participates in it. To encounter Scripture rightly is to encounter the God who speaks and still speaks today.

Teaching and truth

Paul begins his list of Scripture's purposes with teaching. The Word of God educates the people of God. It shapes our whole understanding of who God is, what He has done, and what He calls His people to be. It teaches not merely facts but faith. Scripture instructs us in truth, training the mind to think God's thoughts after Him. *"Your word is a lamp for my feet, a light on my path."* (Psalm 119:105).

The purpose of that light is not to dazzle but to direct - to illuminate the way of obedience. Biblical teaching is more than the transfer of information. It is the cultivation of discernment. God's people are called not just to know His Word but to think with it. The Word forms a worldview - a way of seeing all things through the lens of God's revelation. Without it, believers risk conforming to the patterns of the world rather than the purposes of God.

Paul warns, *"Do not conform to the pattern of this world, but be transformed by the renewing of your mind."* (Romans 12:2). The mind which is renewed by Scripture becomes the instrument of transformation for the whole life.

To teach is to transmit truth that transforms. The early church understood this profoundly. They *"devoted themselves to the apostles' teaching and to fellowship, to the breaking of bread and to prayer."* (Acts 2:42). Teaching was not an academic exercise but an act of worship. To sit under the Word was to submit to its authority and be reshaped by its wisdom. The same remains true today: the purpose of biblical teaching is to bring believers into alignment with the mind and will of God.

Rebuking and correction

If Scripture teaches truth, it must also expose error. The same light that guides also reveals what is wrong. To rebuke is to confront falsehood and wrongdoing; to correct is to restore what has gone astray. Scripture does both with divine precision. *"The word of God is alive and active. Sharper than any double-edged sword, it penetrates even to dividing soul and spirit, joints and marrow; it judges the thoughts and attitudes of the heart."* (Hebrews 4:12). The Bible does not merely challenge behaviour; it discerns motives.

This rebuking and correcting function can be uncomfortable, even painful. It is the spiritual equivalent of surgery - necessary to remove what is diseased so that health may return. God's Word cuts in order to heal. The prophet Nathan's confrontation of David after his sin with Bathsheba is a classic example of Scripture's rebuking power.

Through Nathan, the Word of the Lord pierced the king's hardened conscience: *"You are the man!"* (2 Samuel 12:7). That rebuke led to repentance, and repentance led to restoration.

For the believer, rebuke is never condemnation but invitation. The purpose of correction is not humiliation but transformation. When Scripture confronts us, it is because God is committed to our holiness. His Word is both mirror and medicine: it reveals what is wrong and provides the cure. To submit to the correcting power of Scripture is to open ourselves to divine renewal. Every rebuke, rightly received, becomes a step toward greater freedom.

Training in righteousness

The word *"training"* evokes the discipline of the athlete and the patience of the craftsman. Righteousness is not learned in an instant; it is formed through consistent practice. Scripture provides that training ground. It does not only tell us what is right; it trains us to love what is right. The psalmist declares, *"I have hidden your word in my heart that I might not sin against you."* (Psalm 119:11). To hide the Word is to store it in the soul where it becomes both compass and strength.

Training in righteousness means cultivating habits of obedience. The Word of God shapes character through repetition and reflection. It teaches perseverance when life grows weary, compassion when pride tempts, and humility when success arrives. It trains the conscience to respond to the prompting of the Spirit. Every time the believer reads, prays, and obeys the Word, spiritual muscle is formed.

The Scriptures train not by coercion but by companionship. They walk with us, shaping us over time into the likeness of Christ. This is why consistent engagement with Scripture is essential. Sporadic reading gives information; sustained reading gives formation. The Word of God trains the people of God to live in the way of God. In the end, righteousness is not an achievement but a relationship - the fruit of walking daily with the One whose voice we follow through His Word.

Equipping for every good work

The purpose of Scripture is not merely internal enlightenment but external fruitfulness. God's Word equips His people for *action*. Paul concludes his summary in 2 Timothy by saying that Scripture exists *"so that the servant of God may be thoroughly equipped for every good work."* (2 Timothy 3:17). The Bible trains disciples not just to think rightly but to live rightly. It bridges belief and behaviour, shaping life in service to others.

To be *"equipped"* simply means to be made ready. The Greek term evokes the image of a ship prepared for a long voyage or a soldier fitted with armour. The Word of God furnishes believers with everything necessary for faith and obedience: wisdom for decision-making, courage in times of adversity, and discernment in temptation. Scripture does not just tell us what to do; it forms in us the kind of people who can discern and do what is right.

In the life of the church community, this equipping power becomes communal. The Word equips not only individuals but the whole body of Christ. When pastors preach, when believers teach one another, when families read and pray together, the community is strengthened. The church becomes, in Paul's words, *"built on the foundation of the apostles and prophets, with Christ Jesus himself as the chief cornerstone."* (Ephesians 2:20).

Scripture is the blueprint and the building material for the people of God. The result is a church that not only knows the truth but *embodies* it. In a world adrift in moral confusion, Scripture forms a people of conviction and compassion - those who both proclaim and practise righteousness. The Word equips the saints for service, ensuring that every generation of believers can continue the mission of God with faithfulness and power.

The Word that renews

Scripture's power does not end with instruction or preparation; it renews the inner life of those who receive it. *"The law of the Lord is perfect, refreshing the soul. The statutes of the Lord are trustworthy, making wise the simple."* (Psalm 19:7). The Word of God restores what sin and sorrow erode.

It comforts the weary, strengthens the weak, and revives hope in the discouraged. Unlike any human wisdom, Scripture speaks directly to the deepest needs of the heart because it carries the breath of its Author. Renewal through the Word happens gradually but surely. As believers meditate on Scripture, the Spirit applies it personally, bringing light to confusion and peace to anxiety. This is not mere sentiment but supernatural power at work. Jesus prayed, *"Sanctify them by the truth; your word is truth."* (John 17:17). The Word sanctifies because it connects us to the One who is holy. Each encounter with Scripture is a moment of cleansing, realignment, and re-creation.

The renewing work of Scripture also protects against spiritual stagnation. The Bible continually draws believers back to their first love, correcting drift and rekindling devotion. It confronts cynicism with promise, despair with faith, and pride with humility. Through every season of life, the same Word that once brought us to faith continues to nourish it. The believer who lives by the Word will never run dry, for the Scriptures are an ever-flowing stream of divine life.

The Word that endures

Finally, the power of Scripture lies in its permanence. Human words fade; divine words endure. The prophet declares, *"The grass withers and the flowers fall, but the word of our God endures forever."* (Isaiah 40:8). This endurance is not simply about preservation but about relevance. The truths of Scripture remain as potent today as when they were first written because they reflect the unchanging nature of God.

History has tested the Bible's endurance through persecution, scepticism, and neglect. Yet its influence has never waned. It has outlasted empires, survived suppression, and transformed many civilisations. The Word endures because it is alive - it carries the life of the One who spoke it. To trust Scripture is therefore to anchor life in something that cannot fail. For the believer, the enduring Word is both comfort and commission. It reminds us that God's purposes stand firm through every trial, and it calls us to carry that message into the world.

The same Word that once spoke creation into existence now sustains new creation in the hearts of His people. To live by that Word is to participate in the ongoing work of God Himself.

The Word that reveals Christ

At the heart of the Bible's power and purpose is its revelation of Jesus Christ. Scripture does many things - it instructs, rebukes, encourages - but above all, it points to Him. Jesus Himself declared in John 5:39, *"These are the very Scriptures that testify about me."* The ultimate purpose of the Word is not to provide information but to lead us into relationship with the living Word. From Genesis to Revelation, the entire narrative of Scripture converges in Christ.

In the Law, Christ is the fulfilment; in the Prophets, He is the promise; in the Psalms, He is the song. Every story whispers His name. When the risen Christ walked with the disciples on the road to Emmaus, *"He explained to them what was said in all the Scriptures concerning himself."* (Luke 24:27). The same Spirit who inspired those Scriptures now reveals Christ through them to every believer. The power of the Bible lies not in the paper or ink, but in the Person it unveils.

To read Scripture rightly is to seek Jesus in its pages. The danger of biblical study without this focus is that one may know the text but miss the Truth. The Pharisees memorised the Law but failed to recognise the Lord standing before them. The purpose of Bible reading is not mastery of content but transformation through encounter. When we meet Jesus Christ in the Scripture, the Word becomes life. As Peter confessed in John 6:68, *"You have the words of eternal life."*

The Word and the work of the Spirit

The power of Scripture cannot be separated from the presence of the Spirit. The Word is not self-acting in isolation but operates through the agency of the Holy Spirit, who inspired it and now applies it. The Spirit takes the written Word and makes it the living Word in the hearts of believers.

"The Spirit gives life; the flesh counts for nothing. The words I have spoken to you – they are full of the Spirit and life." (John 6:63). The Spirit's ministry ensures that Scripture never grows stale. A passage read a hundred times can suddenly strike the heart with new power because the Author Himself is present in the reading. Illumination is not the discovery of hidden knowledge but the awakening of spiritual understanding. The same Spirit who hovered over the waters of creation now hovers over the pages of Scripture, bringing light where there was darkness.

This partnership between Word and Spirit protects the church from imbalance. Without the Word, the Spirit's movement could be mistaken for emotion or error; without the Spirit, the Word could become a lifeless text. Together they produce living faith. As Paul told the Thessalonians, *"Our gospel came to you not simply with words but also with power, with the Holy Spirit and deep conviction."* (1 Thessalonians 1:5). The power of the Word is the Spirit's presence within it.

The Word that shapes the church

The church does not stand above Scripture; it stands under it. The Word of God creates, sustains, and governs the people of God. The early church was born through the preaching of the Word, not the authority of an institution. At Pentecost, when Peter proclaimed the gospel, *"those who accepted his message were baptised, and about three thousand were added to their number that day."* (Acts 2:41). The church was founded by the Word, filled by the Spirit, and formed for mission.

Every revival, every reformation, every renewal in church history has been accompanied by a rediscovery of Scripture's authority. When the Word is neglected, faith weakens; when the Word is honoured, faith flourishes. The Scriptures provide the church with its identity and direction. They are not merely a reference point but a lifeline. The Word builds the church by building believers, and it purifies the church by confronting sin and error. To be a biblical church is to be a listening church. We do not edit the Word to suit our times and circumstances; we allow the Word to edit us.

The authority of Scripture is not a heavy burden but a gracious gift - it keeps the community of faith centred on Christ. As Paul wrote to Timothy, *"Preach the word; be prepared in season and out of season; correct, rebuke and encourage - with great patience and careful instruction."* (2 Timothy 4:2). The church that abandons Scripture loses its anchor; the church that listens to Scripture finds its compass.

The Word that discerns and directs

The Bible is not only descriptive but diagnostic. It reads us as we read it. Hebrews declares, *"Nothing in all creation is hidden from God's sight. Everything is uncovered and laid bare before the eyes of him to whom we must give account."*(Hebrews 4:13). The Word of God exposes motives, reveals attitudes, and guides decisions. It is both mirror and map - showing us who we are and where we must go.

In a world of moral confusion and competing voices, Scripture offers clarity. Its authority does not change with opinion or culture because it flows from the unchanging nature of God. The psalmist prays, *"Direct my footsteps according to your word; let no sin rule over me."* (Psalm 119:133). The purpose of the Word is not merely to correct our path but to keep us on it. It trains our instincts, renews our minds, and anchors our convictions.

The discerning power of Scripture also protects against deception. False teaching and spiritual manipulation will thrive where the Word is ignored. The mature believer learns to test every idea, every impulse, every claim against the truth of Scripture. This is not scepticism but faithfulness. The Bereans in Acts 17 were commended because they *"examined the Scriptures every day to see if what Paul said was true."* (Acts 17:11). The same practice remains vital today. The Word not only teaches what is true; it exposes what is false.

The Word that strengthens faith

The Bible does not simply inform believers about God; it nurtures trust in Him. Paul writes, *"Faith comes from hearing the message, and the message is heard through the word about Christ."* (Romans 10:17)

Scripture is the seedbed of faith because it reveals the character and promises of God. The more believers immerse themselves in the Word, the more deeply they learn to rely on Him.

Faith grows through repetition and remembrance. Each time we see God's faithfulness displayed in Scripture, it reinforces our confidence in His unchanging nature. When fear whispers that God has forgotten us, His Word reminds us, *"Never will I leave you; never will I forsake you."* (Hebrews 13:5). When circumstances seem overwhelming, we hear again the assurance, *"The Lord is my light and my salvation - whom shall I fear?"* (Psalm 27:1). Scripture feeds the soul with truth that overcomes lies.

The power of the Word to strengthen faith lies in its living quality. It is not a dead record of past events but a living testimony of ongoing grace. The same God who spoke to Abraham, David, and Paul still speaks today through these pages. His promises are as reliable now as when they were first spoken. To neglect Scripture is to starve faith; to engage with it is to see faith flourish. Every time we open the Bible, God opens His heart.

The Word that transforms the mind

The purpose of Scripture is not merely to change what we believe but to renew how we think. Paul urges believers, *"Do not conform to the pattern of this world, but be transformed by the renewing of your mind."* (Romans 12:2). The Word of God accomplishes that renewal by reorienting our thoughts toward truth. It breaks the power of deception and rewires the mind to perceive reality as God defines it.

This mental transformation has moral and spiritual dimensions. The more we internalise Scripture, the more we think with the mind of Christ. His priorities become ours; His compassion becomes our instinct. The Word reshapes imagination as much as intellect - it teaches us to see the world through the lens of redemption. When Scripture fills the mind, cynicism loses its grip, anxiety loses its power, and self-centredness gives way to Christ-centredness.

The renewing power of the Word also produces discernment. Believers become able to *"test and approve what God's will is -his good, pleasing and perfect will."* (Romans 12:2)

The Bible trains the mind to distinguish between the urgent and the eternal, between human logic and divine wisdom. As the Spirit applies the Word, the believer begins to think God's thoughts after Him - a miracle of grace that continues throughout life.

The Word that forms character

Scripture's power reaches its fullest expression when it shapes who we are, not just what we know. God's intention is to conform believers *"to the image of his Son."* (Romans 8:29). That process happens through the steady influence of His Word.

The stories, psalms, commands, and teachings of Scripture act together as instruments of formation, chiselling the rough edges of human nature into the likeness of Christ.

The fruit of this transformation is moral beauty. The Word cultivates patience, humility, honesty, and courage - the traits of Christ reproduced in His people.

When James describes the *"implanted word, which can save you"* (James 1:21), he portrays Scripture as a living seed that, once rooted, bears fruit in action. True engagement with the Word always results in obedience. As Jesus said, *"Blessed rather are those who hear the word of God and obey it."* (Luke 11:28)

Character formation through Scripture is not automatic but relational. It grows out of daily encounter, listening, repentance, and surrender. Each time the believer says "yes" to the Word, Christ is formed more deeply within.

Over time, Scripture's influence becomes instinctive; it shapes response and reaction, not just reflection. The Bible produces people whose lives themselves become living epistles - letters written not on tablets of stone but on hearts of flesh.

The Word that sends

The power and purpose of Scripture ultimately propel believers outward. The same Word that comforts and corrects also commissions. Jesus' final prayer for His disciples includes this declaration: *"As you sent me into the world, I have sent them into the world."* (John 17:18). The Word that sanctifies also sends. It equips the church not to retreat into safety but to advance with truth.

Mission begins in Bible and flows from it. The Great Commission rests on the authority of the risen Christ who is revealed in the Bible: *"All authority in heaven and on earth has been given to me. Therefore, go and make disciples of all nations."* (Matthew 28:18–19). The power that saves us becomes the power that sends us. The Bible is not only a book to be read but a message to be shared.

When believers take the Word into the world, its power multiplies. Lives are changed, communities are renewed, and the gospel continues to reach the ends of the earth. The same Word that created light still shines into darkness. To live under its authority is to participate in its mission. The purpose of Scripture is fulfilled not only when it is understood but when it is obeyed and proclaimed.

The Word that comforts and confronts

The Bible holds a rare tension - it comforts and confronts in equal measure. In times of grief, it whispers hope; in times of complacency, it calls for repentance. Both are expressions of love. Scripture soothes the wounded and unsettles the self-satisfied, proving that God's Word is alive and active, responding to the condition of the heart.

The psalmist experienced this dual effect: *"When I was a child, my suffering was comforted by your promise."* (Psalm 119:50). Yet that same Word later declares, *"Before I was afflicted, I went astray, but now I obey your word."* (Psalm 119:67). The comfort of Scripture lies in its constancy. God's promises do not shift with emotion or circumstance. In the darkness of despair, His Word shines as a steady flame.

"Even though I walk through the darkest valley, I will fear no evil, for you are with me." (Psalm 23:4). Those who cling to the Word find that its comfort is not sentimental but substantial - rooted in the presence of God Himself. His Word reminds us that we are never abandoned, even when everything else falls away.

Yet that same Word also confronts, challenging our apathy and exposing our idols. The Scriptures speak with prophetic urgency against injustice, hypocrisy, and pride. They comfort the broken but disturb the comfortable. When we open the Bible honestly, we discover that it reads us as much as we read it. Its purpose is not to affirm our assumptions but to align our hearts with God's. The same voice that says, *"Come to me, all you who are weary and burdened,"* also says, *"Take up your cross and follow me."* The Word that heals is also the Word that calls to holiness.

2. The Word that heals the heart

There is a therapeutic power in the Scriptures, but not in the superficial sense of self-help. The Word heals because it will reconnect us to the Healer. *"He sent out his word and healed them; he rescued them from the grave."* (Psalm 107:20). The same creative power that once formed the universe now restores broken souls. God's Word mends what sin fractures - it speaks forgiveness to guilt, truth to confusion, and hope to despair.

When Jesus encountered the centurion who believed that His Word alone could heal, He marvelled at such faith: *"Just say the word, and my servant will be healed."* (Matthew 8:8) That faith captures the essence of biblical confidence. God's Word carries His authority, even when spoken across distance or centuries. Every healing of the heart begins with hearing His Word. The believer who meditates on Scripture drinks from the stream of living water that refreshes the soul and cleanses the conscience.

The Word also heals relationships. Where bitterness and division prevail, Scripture teaches forgiveness and reconciliation. *"Bear with each other and forgive one another if any of you has a grievance against someone. Forgive as the Lord forgave you."* (Colossians 3:13).

The same grace that restores us to God restores us to one another. In this way, the Bible becomes a bridge where hearts long divided by sin can meet again in mercy.

The Word that endures through suffering

The true test of Scripture's power is found in suffering. When everything else collapses, the Word stands. The psalmist affirms, *"If your law had not been my delight, I would have perished in my affliction."* (Psalm 119:92). The promises of God do not remove pain, but they give it purpose. The Bible reframes suffering as a context for faith rather than a contradiction of it.

In Scripture we find not just explanations for suffering but companions in it. Job's cries, David's laments, Jeremiah's tears, and Paul's perseverance reveal that God's Word does not silence pain - it gives it a voice. It can allow lament and hope to coexist. *"Though he slay me, yet will I hope in him."* (Job 13:15). This paradox - trust in the midst of trial — is the essence of biblical faith. The Word gives language to anguish and turns despair into dialogue.

For the believer, the endurance of Scripture mirrors the endurance of God Himself. When the storms of life strip away comfort, the Word remains an anchor. Its promises outlast pain because they are rooted in eternity. Jesus assured His followers, *"Heaven and earth will pass away, but my words will never pass away."* (Matthew 24:35). The durability of the Word ensures that those who cling to it will never be without hope.

The Word that unites

Scripture also possesses the remarkable power to unite what sin divides. Humanity's divisions - ethnic, social, generational - find reconciliation under the authority of the same Word. In the early church, Jews and Gentiles, rich and poor, men and women were bound together by the gospel's truth. Paul proclaimed, *"There is neither Jew nor Gentile, neither slave nor free, nor is there male and female, for you are all one in Christ Jesus."* (Galatians 3:28). The Word that reveals our equality before God also teaches our unity in Him.

The Bible unites not by erasing differences but by elevating Christ above them. The shared submission to His Word creates fellowship stronger than culture or preference. When the people of God gather around Scripture, barriers break and belonging begins. The same Spirit who inspired the Word also creates community through it. The church is healthiest when it listens together to the voice of God, allowing the Word to be the final authority in faith and practice.

This unifying power has always been part of God's design. From the beginning, His Word gathered creation into harmony: light with darkness, sea with sky, man with woman. Sin fractured that unity; the gospel restores it. In the new creation, the redeemed will once again be one people under one Word. Until that day, every time believers open the Scriptures together, they practise that coming harmony - the foretaste of eternal fellowship around the throne where the Lamb Himself is the living Word.

The Word that judges and justifies

The same Word that comforts and heals also judges. This is not contradiction but completeness. The Word of God exposes sin precisely so that it can extend mercy. Jesus declared, *"The very words I have spoken will condemn them at the last day."* (John 12:48). The Word serves as the standard of truth, revealing the moral order by which every life will one day be measured. Scripture does not just offer guidance; it proclaims accountability.

Yet judgment in Scripture always carries redemptive intent. God exposes sin not to destroy but to deliver. The same Word that convicts also offers pardon through Christ. In Romans 8:1, Paul affirms, *"There is now no condemnation for those who are in Christ Jesus."* The Bible's power lies in this paradox: the Word that declares guilt also announces grace. When the sinner hears and believes, judgment becomes justification, and law gives way to love. This dual function keeps the believer humble and hopeful. We read the Scriptures not as critics standing above them but as those standing beneath their light. The Word judges our motives so that grace may renew our hearts. It is both mirror and mercy seat. Every conviction of sin is an invitation to restoration.

The same God who once said *"Let there be light"* now speaks into the shadows of human hearts, creating new life through the gospel's declaration of forgiveness.

The Word that inspires worship

The ultimate purpose of Scripture is worship. The Bible does not end in information or even transformation but in adoration. When we encounter God through His Word, the natural response is praise. The psalmist exclaims, *"I rejoice in your promise like one who finds great spoil."* (Psalm 119:162). The discovery of divine truth brings delight. The more we understand the Scriptures, the more we are moved to worship the Author.

Worship arises when truth ignites the heart. The Bible reveals God's majesty, mercy, and faithfulness, and in response the believer bows in wonder. Every page of Scripture is an invitation to behold His glory. The prophet Jeremiah expressed this joy: *"When your words came, I ate them; they were my joy and my heart's delight."* (Jeremiah 15:16). The Word nourishes worship because it feeds the soul with the reality of God's goodness.

Scripture-centred worship keeps the church alive. Without the Word, worship becomes emotion without foundation; with the Word, it becomes spirit and truth. Jesus told the Samaritan woman, *"True worshippers will worship the Father in the Spirit and in truth."* (John 4:23). The Word provides that truth; the Spirit supplies that life. Together they transform worship from ritual into encounter. The power of Scripture culminates when the people of God respond with gratitude, reverence, and obedience.

The Word that sends us back into the world

The Bible never allows faith to become inward-looking. Those who are shaped by Scripture are sent into the world to embody its message. The Word that gathers the church also scatters it for mission. James reminds us, *"Do not merely listen to the word, and so deceive yourselves. Do what it says."* (James 1:22). The measure of biblical engagement is not how much we know but how faithfully we live.

Scripture propels believers into action because it reveals God's heart for the world. From the call of Abraham to the Great Commission, the pattern is the same: God speaks so that His people may go. The Word equips, energises, and empowers the church to be salt and light. It transforms private devotion into public witness.

Isaiah heard the divine call, *"Whom shall I send? And who will go for us?"* He responded, *"Here am I. Send me!"* (Isaiah 6:8). Every believer shaped by the Word eventually hears that same call.

When the church lives out Scripture, the world sees the gospel in motion. Acts of compassion, justice, and mercy become visible expressions of the written Word. The power of Scripture extends beyond the page when its truth is embodied in daily life. The Bible is not a retreat from reality but the revelation that equips us to engage it. Its purpose is fulfilled when its readers become its messengers.

The Word that endures forever

The final word on Scripture is the same as the Scripture's own testimony: it endures. *"The grass withers and the flowers fall, but the word of our God endures forever."* (Isaiah 40:8). Its power does not depend on human acceptance or cultural approval. Kings have banned it, critics have mocked it, and empires have tried to silence it - yet it remains. The Bible's endurance is not merely historical but eternal. Its truth will stand when every earthly power has passed away.

To live by the Word is to invest in eternity. The Scriptures that guide our steps today will one day be fulfilled in sight, when faith becomes vision and the written Word gives way to the Living Word Himself. Until then, believers walk by the light of this revelation, finding in its pages the voice of the eternal God who still speaks. The Bible's power lies not only in what it says but in what it does: it draws humanity back to its Creator, renews hearts, and sustains hope until all things are made new. The power and purpose of Scripture converge in one truth: it is the means by which God accomplishes His will among His people.

5. THE TRUSTWORTHINESS OF THE BIBLE

A question as old as faith

From the very beginning, humanity has been confronted with one recurring question: *Can God be trusted?* The serpent's first words to Eve in Genesis 3:1, were not a direct denial of God's existence but a subtle attack on His reliability: *"Did God really say...?"* That ancient question still echoes today in countless forms of doubt about Scripture's truth, authority, and relevance. Every generation faces the temptation to question whether the Bible can be taken at its word.

Yet the entire life of faith depends on the answer. If God has spoken, and if His Word is true, then everything else - our worship, our obedience, our mission - from that confidence. But if Scripture is unreliable, faith collapses into speculation. The trustworthiness of the Bible, therefore, is not a peripheral issue; it is the foundation of Christian conviction. To trust God is to trust His Word. The two cannot be separated.

The Bible never defends its truthfulness with human argument - it simply declares it. *"Every word of God is flawless; he is a shield to those who take refuge in him."* (Proverbs 30:5). The Word does not require our validation; it invites our submission. But God, in His grace, has provided abundant evidence for us - historical, prophetic, experiential, and spiritual – the prove the Scriptures are indeed trustworthy. To explore that evidence is not an act of scepticism – it is an act of worship.

The character of God

The ultimate reason the Bible can be trusted is not found in archaeology or manuscript evidence, but in the character of its Author. Scripture reflects the nature of the God who breathed it. Because He is truthful, His Word is true. Because He is faithful, His promises endure. *"God is not human, that he should lie, not a human being, that he should change his mind."* (Numbers 23:19). The trustworthiness of the Bible begins with the trustworthiness of God Himself.

This is why every attack on Scripture ultimately becomes an attack on the divine character. To question the truth of the Word is to question the integrity of the One who spoke it. But history and experience consistently affirm that God is faithful to His Word. He has never failed to keep a promise. The psalmist could therefore testify, *"Your word, Lord, is eternal; it stands firm in the heavens."* (Psalm 119:89). The unchanging nature of God always guarantees the enduring truth of His revelation.

Because God's nature is always consistent, His Word is coherent. Across centuries, languages, and cultures, the Bible speaks with remarkable unity about the human condition and the divine solution. From Genesis to Revelation, one story unfolds – it is the story of creation, the fall, and then redemption and restoration. The consistency of that message, written by dozens of human authors over more than a millennium, bears witness to one divine mind behind it all.

The testimony of Jesus

The credibility of Scripture also rests on the authority of Jesus Christ. If we call Him Lord, we must regard the Scriptures as He did. Jesus consistently affirmed the divine inspiration and reliability of the Old Testament. He declared, *"Scripture cannot be set aside."* (John 10:35). He treated its words as authoritative, binding, and final. In His temptation in the wilderness, Jesus responded to Satan's challenges not with personal reasoning but with the repeated declaration, *"It is written."* (Matthew 4:4). Whilst on earth, the Son of God Himself actually lived under the authority of the written Word.

Jesus' confidence in Scripture was absolute. He stated, *"Until heaven and earth disappear, not the smallest letter, not the least stroke of a pen, will by any means disappear from the Law until everything is accomplished."* (Matthew 5:18). Such reverence for the text leaves no room for the idea that Scripture might be partially inspired or occasionally mistaken. For Jesus, to believe in the Father was to believe the Word the Father had given. Moreover, Jesus authenticated the prophetic and historical truth of Scripture through His life, death, and resurrection.

He fulfilled the very prophecies He endorsed. After His resurrection, He reminded the disciples, *"Everything must be fulfilled that is written about me in the Law of Moses, the Prophets and the Psalms."* (Luke 24:44). The reliability of Scripture and the reality of Christ's resurrection stand or fall together. To trust Jesus is to trust the Bible He trusted.

The witness of the Apostles

The early church inherited from Jesus the same unwavering conviction about Scriptural truth. The apostles did not see the Bible as one sacred text among many but as the unique, God-breathed revelation of divine truth.

We see in 2 Peter 1:21, where Peter affirmed, *"Prophecy never had its origin in the human will, but prophets, though human, spoke from God as they were carried along by the Holy Spirit."* The human authors were instruments, not inventors. Inspiration did not erase their individuality, but it ensured their accuracy.

The apostolic writings themselves were received as Scripture because they carried the same divine authority. Paul claimed that his words were not merely his own but the Lord's: *"We also thank God continually because, when you received the word of God, which you heard from us, you accepted it not as a human word, but as it actually is, the word of God."* (1 Thessalonians 2:13).

We can therefore see that the early believers recognised in these writings the same Spirit who had spoken through the prophets.

By the time the New Testament canon began to take shape, the church was not deciding which books were authoritative but recognising which ones already bore the mark of divine origin.

The consistency of doctrine, the authenticity of apostolic witness, and the transforming power of the message confirmed that these were indeed the words of God. The trustworthiness of the Bible is therefore grounded not in human decision but in divine inspiration.

The unity of Scripture

Perhaps the strongest evidence for the trustworthiness of the Bible is its remarkable unity. Written over a span of about fifteen hundred years by more than forty authors - kings and shepherds, prophets and fishermen, scholars and tax collectors - the Bible nevertheless tells one coherent story. It begins with creation, ends with new creation, and in between reveals the unfolding plan of redemption centred in Jesus Christ.

This unity cannot be explained by coincidence or conspiracy. The authors lived in different eras, spoke different languages, and came from vastly different backgrounds, yet their writings converge on the same truth: the faithfulness of God and the salvation of humanity.

The Old Testament anticipates what the New Testament fulfils. Shadows give way to substance; promises find their fulfilment and completion. The thread of grace runs unbroken from Genesis to Revelation, binding every book into one divine tapestry.

The harmony of Scripture stands in contrast to the disunity of human philosophies. While the world's ideas shift and collide, the Bible's message remains consistent. It does not need revision to fit modern insight because it transcends time and culture. Its moral vision, spiritual coherence, and prophetic accuracy reveal a single Author guiding the whole. As Peter declared, *"The word of the Lord endures forever."* (1 Peter 1:25)

The fulfilment of prophecy

Another powerful confirmation of Scripture's reliability is the fulfilment of prophecy. Unlike the vague predictions of human speculation, biblical prophecy is very detailed, it's historical, and it is verifiable. Through it, God demonstrates that His Word stands above time. *"I make known the end from the beginning, from ancient times, what is still to come."* (Isaiah 46:10). Prophecy is God's signature across history - evidence that He alone holds the future.

The life of Jesus provides the most compelling example. His birth, ministry, death, and resurrection fulfilled hundreds of Old Testament prophecies with astonishing precision. Micah foretold His birthplace in Bethlehem (Micah 5:2). Isaiah described His suffering and substitutionary death (Isaiah 53). Zechariah anticipated the betrayal of Jesus for just thirty pieces of silver (Zechariah 11:12–13). These and many others converged in the life of one man who lived centuries later.

Mathematical probability alone rules out coincidence. The fulfilment of prophecy confirms that Scripture is not a random collection of human ideas but the outworking of divine intention. What God promises, He performs. Each fulfilled prophecy builds a stronger bridge of trust from the written Word to the living experience of faith. The God who kept His word in the past can be trusted to keep it in the present.

The preservation of the text

Critics often question whether the Bible we read today accurately reflects the original writings. Yet the evidence for its preservation is stronger than for any other ancient document. Thousands of different manuscripts - Hebrew, Greek, and early translations – all confirm that the text has been transmitted with extraordinary care.

The discovery of the Dead Sea Scrolls in the twentieth century, for example, revealed that the Hebrew Scriptures copied a thousand years earlier matched the later Masoretic Text almost word for word.

This meticulous preservation is no accident; it is providence. God not only inspired His Word but also safeguarded it. *"The words of the Lord are flawless, like silver purified in a crucible, like gold refined seven times. You, Lord, will keep the needy safe and will protect us forever from the wicked."* (Psalm 12:6–7). Across centuries of persecution, censorship, and neglect, the Scriptures have survived intact, defying the fate of countless other ancient writings.

Even translations, often cited as a source of distortion, has served to extend rather than dilute the Word's influence. From the Septuagint to the Reformation and beyond, translation has carried the message of Scripture into new languages and cultures while preserving its essential meaning. The same Spirit who inspired the original text continues to oversee its faithful transmission, ensuring that the voice of God remains clear to every generation.

The power of transformation

Perhaps the most compelling evidence for the trustworthiness of the Bible lies not in manuscripts or prophecies but in changed lives. For more than two millennia, Scripture has transformed individuals and societies in ways no other book has achieved. It has liberated the oppressed, reformed laws, inspired art, and kindled faith in hearts across every culture. Its words have guided saints, strengthened martyrs, and comforted the dying. This transformative power is not psychological suggestion but divine encounter.

The apostle Paul described it plainly: *"The gospel is the power of God that brings salvation to everyone who believes."*(Romans 1:16). That power continues today wherever the Word is read and received. No other text consistently produces repentance, hope, and holiness. The same Scripture that once turned Saul the persecutor into Paul the apostle continues to turn sceptics into servants. Its reliability is proved by its results.

The enduring impact of Scripture cannot be accounted for by human genius. Literature may move emotions, philosophy may challenge intellect, but only the Word of God changes hearts. The Bible's trustworthiness is ultimately verified in the lives of those who trust it. Every believer who has been born again through its message stands as living proof that the Word of God is true.

The Bible and history

The trustworthiness of Scripture is reinforced by its deep roots in verifiable history. Unlike myth or legend, the Bible anchors its narrative in time and place.

Its events unfold amid real empires, kings, and nations that archaeology continues to uncover. The names and locations that fill its pages are not the inventions of religious imagination but the coordinates of history itself. Luke begins his Gospel by asserting that his account is based on *"eyewitnesses and servants of the word,"* written *"so that you may know the certainty of the things you have been taught."* (Luke 1:2–4)

Archaeology has confirmed the Bible's historical reliability again and again. Once-dismissed figures such as Pontius Pilate, King David, and Belshazzar have all been verified through various inscriptions and discoveries. Ancient cities thought mythical - Nineveh, Jericho, and Sodom - have been unearthed, their ruins bearing silent witness to the accuracy of the biblical record. These findings do not create faith, but they confirm that the faith is grounded in fact. The Scriptures do not float in abstraction; they stand firmly within human history.

This historical foundation distinguishes the Bible from other sacred texts. Christianity is not built upon private revelation or philosophical speculation but upon public events witnessed and recorded. As Peter proclaimed, *"We did not follow cleverly devised stories when we told you about the coming of our Lord Jesus Christ in power, but we were eyewitnesses of his majesty."* (2 Peter 1:16). The gospel is historical truth interpreted by divine revelation, not myth clothed in piety.

The Bible and science

Some critics have argued that modern science undermines the credibility of Scripture, yet history tells a different story. Far from being opposed to scientific discovery, the Bible provided the worldview that made science possible. It revealed a universe created by a rational God who ordered nature with consistency, making observation and experimentation meaningful. Without the biblical conviction that creation is orderly and intelligible, science itself would have no foundation. Many of the pioneers of modern science - Kepler, Newton, Pascal, Faraday - were all very devoted students of Scripture. They saw no conflict between faith and reason because they understood that both flowed from the same Source.

The Bible does not seek to be a textbook of science but a revelation of truth about God, humanity, and the moral order. Where Scripture speaks of nature, it does so truthfully, even if not in technical modern terms. The psalmist writes, *"The heavens declare the glory of God; the skies proclaim the work of his hands."* (Psalm 19:1). Science explores the mechanism; Scripture reveals the meaning.

When properly interpreted, the Bible and science complement rather than contradict each other. Apparent tensions often arise not from what the Bible says but from human assumptions about what it must mean. The purpose of the Bible is not to tell us how the heavens go, but how to go to heaven. Its authority concerns ultimate realities - why creation exists, who sustains it, and how redemption enters it. The more we learn about the natural world, the more reason we find to marvel at the God who designed it.

The Bible and reason

Faith and reason are not enemies but allies. The Bible invites rigorous thought, calling believers to love God *"with all your mind."* (Matthew 22:37). True faith is never blind; it is informed trust based on evidence of God's faithfulness. The Scriptures engage reason by offering coherent explanations of reality - of human nature, morality, meaning, and destiny - that surpass any competing worldview.

Far from discouraging inquiry, the Bible encourages it. The Bereans were commended because they *"examined the Scriptures every day to see if what Paul said was true."* (Acts 17:11). Christianity welcomes investigation because it is grounded in truth, not superstition. When faith is examined honestly, it grows stronger, not weaker. The same Word that calls us to believe also calls us to think. The integration of faith and intellect has fuelled centuries of education, ethics, and exploration.

The rational coherence of the Bible itself is a testimony to divine authorship. Across thousands of verses, written by dozens of authors, the Bible maintains consistency about the nature of God and the moral order of creation.

Its worldview accounts for both the grandeur and the brokenness of humanity in a way that satisfies both the heart and the intellect. Reason alone cannot produce revelation, but revelation makes reason whole. Faith does not silence the mind; it sanctifies it.

The Bible and morality

The ethical power of Scripture provides another proof of its reliability. The moral vision it presents is not arbitrary or culturally bound but rooted in the very character of God. His commands reflect who He is - holy, just, and loving. The Ten Commandments, the Sermon on the Mount, and the letters of Paul reveal a moral order that both transcends and transforms cultures. This constancy across time demonstrates that biblical morality is not a human construct but a divine revelation.

The moral wisdom of the Bible has shaped civilisations. Concepts such as human dignity, equality before the law, compassion for the poor, and the sanctity of life all trace their origins to Scripture. Even those who reject its authority often borrow from its moral capital. Jesus summarised the entire law in two commands: *"Love the Lord your God with all your heart and with all your soul and with all your mind… and love your neighbour as yourself."* (Matthew 22:37–39). No ethical system has ever improved upon this simplicity or power.

The consistency of the Bible's moral message reinforces its divine origin. Human ethics evolve with opinion; divine truth endures. The same standards that applied in ancient Israel still speak today because they arise from the unchanging holiness of God. When people live by these truths, societies flourish; when they abandon them, chaos follows.

The Bible and experience

Beyond external evidence and intellectual argument, the Bible proves itself through experience. Millions of believers across centuries testify that when they read the Scriptures, something happens - hearts are pierced, burdens are lifted, and direction is found.

The writer of Hebrews describes this living dynamic: *"The word of God is alive and active. Sharper than any double-edged sword, it penetrates even to dividing soul and spirit, joints and marrow; it judges the thoughts and attitudes of the heart."* (Hebrews 4:12). The Bible not only speaks about God; it speaks from God.

The experiential trustworthiness of Scripture lies in its ability to reach every person in every condition. To the sinner it brings conviction; to the broken it offers comfort; to the weary it gives hope. Its wisdom proves timeless because it addresses the human heart at its deepest level. The shepherd on the hills of Judah, the exile in Babylon, the merchant in Corinth, and the believer today all find themselves described in its pages. The universality of its relevance is itself a miracle.

Those who doubt the Bible's truth are often persuaded not by argument but by encounter. When the Word is opened, the Spirit bears witness within, confirming that these words are divine. Jesus promised, *"The Advocate, the Holy Spirit, whom the Father will send in my name, will teach you all things and will remind you of everything I have said to you."* (John 14:26). This inward assurance does not replace reason or evidence - it completes them. The believer's confidence in Scripture is both rationally supported and spiritually confirmed.

The Bible and the church

Throughout history, the church has stood as a living testimony to the reliability of the Word. It was born through the preaching of Scripture and sustained by its promises. Whenever the church has flourished, it has done so under the authority of the Bible; whenever it has faltered, it has drifted from it. The pattern is unmistakable. Reformation, revival, and renewal have always followed a return to Scripture.

The continuity of Christian witness across centuries also attests to the Bible's truth. Despite divisions of denomination and culture, believers around the world unite in confessing the same core message derived from Scripture: that Jesus Christ is Lord, crucified for sin, risen from the dead, and reigning forever.

The survival of this confession across persecution, exile, and doubt shows that the Word which birthed it cannot be destroyed. As Jesus declared, *"Heaven and earth will pass away, but my words will never pass away."* (Matthew 24:35)

The Bible also continues to prove itself in the life of the church today. Its teaching guides worship, shapes doctrine, and defines mission. Through its pages the Spirit still calls, convicts, and commissions. Each sermon preached, each prayer answered, each conversion witnessed is another testimony to the enduring reliability of God's Word. The church is not the guardian of the Bible; the Bible is the guardian of the church.

The Bible and opposition

Ironically, even the Bible's opponents have helped prove its endurance. No other book in history has been so banned, burned, or ridiculed - yet none has survived with such vitality. Empires have tried to erase it, sceptics have predicted its demise, and critics have declared it obsolete, but the Word of God continues to thrive. Voltaire once boasted that within a century Christianity would be forgotten, yet his own home later became a storehouse for Bibles. The Scripture's survival defies human explanation.

This resilience fulfils God's promise through Isaiah: *"So is my word that goes out from my mouth: It will not return to me empty, but will accomplish what I desire and achieve the purpose for which I sent it."* (Isaiah 55:11). The more the Bible is attacked, the more it proves indestructible. Persecution has scattered its pages into new lands; scepticism has driven deeper study and greater discovery. The Word endures not because of human effort but because of divine preservation.

Opposition also reveals the power of the message. Falsehood rarely provokes such persistent hostility. The reason Scripture stirs resistance is that it confronts human pride and exposes moral rebellion. Yet for every critic silenced by time, another believer will rise up to proclaim its truth. The Bible does not need defence; it simply needs declaration. As Charles Spurgeon once said, *"Defend the Bible? I would as soon defend a lion. Just open the cage and let it roar."*

The Bible and the enduring Word

When all arguments have been made and all evidence examined, the trustworthiness of the Bible rests on one enduring reality - the Word of the living God. Every generation rediscovers that truth anew within the pages of the Bible. Those who trust it find it trustworthy. Those who test it find it unbreakable. Its promises never fail because its Author never lies. *"Your word, Lord, is eternal; it stands firm in the heavens."* (Psalm 119:89)

The Bible's preservation through time, its coherence across cultures, its fulfilment in history, and its transformation of lives all converge to bear one witness: this is no ordinary book. It is the revelation of the God who cannot fail. To doubt it is to doubt Him; to believe it is to rest upon the Rock of ages. The Christian who builds his life on Scripture stands upon solid ground, unshaken by the shifting sands of culture or scepticism.

The Word that has survived fire, exile, and ridicule will stand until the end of time. Jesus prayed, *"Sanctify them by the truth; your word is truth."* (John 17:17). That same truth continues to sanctify, strengthen, and sustain His people today.

The trustworthiness of the Bible is not merely an article of faith; it is the lived experience of the church through the ages. To open its pages is to hear the voice of God - and that voice can be trusted forever.

The Word proven in daily life

The trustworthiness of the Bible is not confined to academic debate or theological argument - it is proven in the crucible of daily life. Every believer who builds their life upon Scripture discovers that its promises hold true in the most ordinary and the most extraordinary circumstances.

The psalmist could testify, *"I have been young and now am old, yet I have never seen the righteous forsaken or their children begging bread."* (Psalm 37:25). That is not the voice of theory, it is the voice of experience.

In times of joy, the Bible interprets our gratitude; in times of sorrow, it steadies our soul. When the world shakes, the Bible remains unshaken. It proves itself in the hospital ward, the battlefield, the prison cell, and the quiet faithfulness of those who pray in secret. The Bible has sustained missionaries in exile, comforted martyrs in flames, and strengthened countless other believers facing loss and fear and death. Such endurance cannot be explained by sentiment - it is evidence of divine origin.

Scripture is not only trustworthy because it is true; it is true because it works. Its principles produce peace, its commands foster justice, and its promises impart hope. The one who obeys it discovers that God's wisdom is not abstract but practical. As the Psalmist reminds us, *"The statutes of the Lord are trustworthy, making wise the simple."* (Psalm 19:7). The ordinary Christian who takes that verse literally soon learns that the Bible's reliability is not limited to the scholar's study - it is lived out in the believer's daily walk.

The reliability of revelation

The Bible is trustworthy because revelation itself is reliable. If God desires to make Himself known - and Scripture declares that He does - then we can trust that He has communicated clearly and faithfully. Divine revelation is not dependent on human brilliance but on divine initiative. *"The secret things belong to the Lord our God, but the things revealed belong to us and to our children forever."* (Deuteronomy 29:29). God has spoken, and He has spoken in a way that can be understood.

This truth rescues believers from the despair of relativism. In a world that insists all truth is subjective, the Bible anchors us in objective revelation. God has not left humanity groping in darkness but has illuminated the path of righteousness. The Scriptures are not a record of human guesses about God; they are God's gracious disclosure of Himself to humanity. They do not contain fragments of truth mixed with error - they are, as Jesus declared, *"Your word is truth."* (John 17:17). If God could not reveal Himself reliably, He would not be God.

The trustworthiness of the Bible therefore rests on the perfection of divine communication. Just as creation reveals our God's power through order and beauty, so Scripture reveals His mind through clarity and coherence. The same Spirit who inspired the prophets and apostles also enlightens readers today, ensuring that God's message is not lost across languages or generations. Revelation is reliable because the Revealer is faithful.

The Bible and the Reliability of transmission

Some wonder whether the Bible has been corrupted through centuries of copying and translation. Yet the evidence of textual reliability remains overwhelming. The ancient scribes of Israel were meticulous in their transcription of the Hebrew Scriptures, counting every letter and word to preserve accuracy. Early Christian copyists carried the same reverence into the Greek manuscripts of the New Testament, resulting in thousands of surviving copies that agree with remarkable consistency.

Modern textual criticism, far from undermining confidence in the Bible, has strengthened it. The comparison of many ancient manuscripts - such as the *Codex Sinaiticus, Codex Vaticanus,* and the Dead Sea Scrolls - reveals a text astonishingly stable over time. Differences among manuscripts are usually just minor variations in spelling or word order, none of which affect essential doctrine. The God who inspired His Word has also preserved it. *"Heaven and earth will pass away, but my words will never pass away."* (Matthew 24:35)

Translation, too, demonstrates the resilience of divine truth. The Word of God has crossed linguistic and cultural boundaries without losing its essence. Whether read in Greek, Latin, English, Swahili, or Mandarin, the message remains the same: salvation through faith in Christ alone.

The Bible is not bound by geography or language because its Author transcends both. The consistency of meaning across multiple translations attests to the Spirit's ongoing guardianship of the text.

The reliability of interpretation

The trustworthiness of Scripture also depends on its faithful interpretation. The Bible is clear in its essentials, yet deep enough to engage a lifetime of study. Its reliability is not diminished by the diversity of interpretation; rather, its depth invites careful exploration under the guidance of the Holy Spirit. *"The Spirit of truth... will guide you into all the truth."* (John 16:13). Illumination ensures that believers can grasp the truth that saves and live by the truth that sanctifies.

Misinterpretation does not disprove reliability - it demonstrates the need for humility. The danger lies not in the text but in the reader who imposes personal bias upon it. That is why Scripture must interpret Scripture, and why community reading within the church guards against individual distortion. The same Spirit who inspired the Word indwells the people of God, creating collective discernment. When the church listens together, truth prevails over speculation.

Faithful interpretation begins with reverence. The Bible is not a puzzle to solve but a revelation to receive. The reader who approaches the Bible prayerfully, seeking obedience rather than confirmation, will find it trustworthy. In 1 Corinthians 2:14–15, Paul wrote, *"The man without the Spirit does not accept the things that come from the Spirit of God... but the spiritual man makes judgments about all things."* The trustworthiness of Scripture becomes evident not merely in what it says but in what it does - it leads those who study it with faith into deeper truth.

The reliability of application

The final measure of trustworthiness lies in how the Bible works when obeyed. It has proven true not only in what it teaches but in what it accomplishes. When its principles are followed, lives are healed, relationships are restored, and societies flourish. The teachings of Jesus on forgiveness, humility, generosity, and love have transformed cultures and hearts across the ages. The Word of God proves itself by its fruit. *"By their fruit you will recognise them."* (Matthew 7:16)

Consider how biblical truth reshapes moral character. Those who take Scripture seriously find their priorities reordered and their desires purified. Pride yields to humility, resentment to mercy, greed to contentment. The Beatitudes describe a kind of person the world cannot produce by its own strength - poor in spirit yet rich in grace, meek yet mighty in love. The Bible does not simply prescribe behaviour; it produces transformation. The more its commands are lived out, the more its truth is vindicated. The same is true in society. Wherever Scripture has taken root, it has elevated the value of human life, advanced education, defended the oppressed, and promoted compassion. Hospitals, schools, and charities all trace their origins to biblical conviction. These are not accidental by-products; they are the natural outcome of a worldview grounded in the truth of God's Word. History confirms that when Scripture shapes culture, justice and mercy flourish; when it is rejected, chaos and cruelty follow.

The reliability of the Spirit

The ultimate assurance of the Bible's trustworthiness comes from the Holy Spirit Himself. The same Spirit who inspired the Word confirms it in the hearts of true believers. In Romans 8:16, Paul says, *"The Spirit himself testifies with our spirit that we are God's children."* This inward testimony extends to the Scriptures. The Spirit bears witness that these words are divine and dependable. This is why faith in the Bible's truth is not blind credulity but Spirit-given conviction.

The Spirit does not bypass reason or evidence but strengthens them. He illumines the mind to recognise truth when it is encountered. Without His work, the Bible may appear as mere literature; with His illumination, it becomes living revelation. The inward witness of the Spirit transforms belief from opinion into certainty. As John wrote, *"You have an anointing from the Holy One, and all of you know the truth."* (1 John 2:20)

This assurance produces in us both confidence and humility. Confidence, because the believer stands on the unshakable Word of God; humility, because this knowledge is a gift of grace, not an achievement of intellect.

The Spirit confirms that Scripture is trustworthy not through argument alone but through encounter. As believers read, obey, and experience its promises fulfilled, they find that the Word is indeed what it claims to be - alive, effective, and eternal.

The Word that endures forever

The trustworthiness of the Bible culminates in its endurance!
"The grass withers and the flowers fall, but the word of our God endures forever." (Isaiah 40:8). No other book has been copied, translated, quoted, and distributed on such a scale. It has survived the rise and fall of empires, the attacks of sceptics, and the apathy of generations. Its longevity is not a coincidence but a confirmation that it carries the breath of eternity.

Every attempt to suppress Scripture has ultimately failed. The Word has outlived its persecutors and converted its critics. It remains relevant not because it adapts to every age but because it transcends them all. The Bible does not depend on culture to validate it; rather, it judges culture with divine authority. It speaks as clearly to the digital age as it did to the ancient world, for its Author is the same yesterday, today, and forever.

This endurance invites a response. To know that the Bible is trustworthy is not enough; we must trust it. The same Word that stood firm through millennia must now be allowed to stand at the centre of our lives. Its promises are true, its warnings real, its hope secure. The believer who builds upon it stands unshaken, for Christ Himself is the foundation upon which every word must rest.

The Word and the final promise

Ultimately, the Bible's trustworthiness points beyond itself to the One who is the living Word. Jesus Christ embodies all that Scripture proclaims. To trust the Bible is to trust Him. The final promise of Scripture is not merely information about the future but the assurance of eternal life in His presence. *"These are written that you may believe that Jesus is the Messiah, the Son of God, and that by believing you may have life in his name."* (John 20:31)

That purpose defines every page of the Bible. Its laws reveal our need; its prophecies reveal His plan; its Gospels reveal His person; its letters reveal His power. Every word leads us to faith in Christ, and every promise finds its "Yes" in Him. The Bible is trustworthy because He is. Its authority is not abstract but personal - it flows from the faithfulness of the risen Lord who still speaks through it.

When history ends and faith becomes sight, the written Word will give way to the living Word in full glory. Yet even then, its truth will not fade. The Scriptures will stand as eternal testimony to God's faithfulness. Until that day, we hold them close, knowing that every word is trustworthy and true. *"For the word of the Lord is right and true; he is faithful in all he does."* (Psalm 33:4)

6. THE SPIRIT AND THE WORD

The Spirit who speaks through Scripture

From the opening chapters of Genesis to the final words of Revelation, the Bible presents the Holy Spirit not as a distant observer but as the divine communicator of God's Word. *"All Scripture is God-breathed and is useful for teaching, rebuking, correcting and training in righteousness."* (2 Timothy 3:16). The breath of God that inspired the writers is the same breath that brings understanding to readers today.

The phrase *God-breathed* reveals the Spirit's intimate role. Just as breath animates the human body, the Spirit animates the written Word. Scripture is not a relic of divine communication but a living conduit. *"For prophecy never had its origin in the human will, but prophets, though human, spoke from God as they were carried along by the Holy Spirit."* (2 Peter 1:21). The Bible's authority and power flow from this origin - it is not simply about God; it is from God.

This means that reading Scripture without the Spirit's illumination is like admiring the cover of a closed book. The text remains the same, but its life and light are veiled. The Spirit who inspired the Word must also interpret it. Theologians have often said that the Bible is *"the only book whose Author is always present when it is read."* This is not poetic exaggeration but spiritual fact. The Holy Spirit meets every believer in the act of reading, guiding, convicting, comforting, and revealing Christ afresh.

The Spirit as the divine Interpreter

One of the greatest misunderstandings of Scripture arises when readers treat it as merely human literature. The Bible must be read with the same Spirit by whom it was written. Paul declared, *"What we have received is not the spirit of the world, but the Spirit who is from God, so that we may understand what God has freely given us."* (1 Corinthians 2:12). Intellectual study is valuable, but without the Spirit, it can become sterile. Only the Spirit can turn information into revelation.

This is why two people may read the same Bible passage and respond entirely differently - one leaves unchanged, the other transformed. The difference lies not in the text but in the presence of the Interpreter. The Spirit does not add new meaning to Scripture; He unveils the meaning that was always there. He bridges the gap between ancient words and present hearts. Through the Holy Spirit, the eternal Word speaks personally and powerfully in every generation.

The Spirit's illumination also guards the church against error. Left to human interpretation alone, Scripture could be twisted to justify almost anything. But the Spirit anchors meaning in divine intent. He reminds readers that the Bible was given not for speculation but for sanctification. *"When he, the Spirit of truth, comes, he will guide you into all the truth."*(John 16:13). The Spirit's role is not to entertain the curious but to transform the faithful.

The Word and the wind

The Hebrew word *ruach* and the Greek word *pneuma* both mean "spirit," "breath," or "wind." This linguistic link reveals the living relationship between Scripture and the Spirit. When the Bible is read in faith, the wind of God's Spirit moves again, bringing life to what was lifeless and clarity to what was confused. *"The words I have spoken to you - they are full of the Spirit and life."* (John 6:63)

The connection between the Word and the Spirit can be seen in Ezekiel's vision of the valley of dry bones. God commanded the prophet to speak to lifeless skeletons: *"Prophesy to these bones and say to them, 'Dry bones, hear the word of the Lord!'"* (Ezekiel 37:4). As Ezekiel obeyed, breath entered them, and they lived. The Word was spoken, but the Spirit gave life. The same miracle occurs whenever the Scriptures are proclaimed in the Spirit's power - dead hearts awaken, faith rises, and lives are restored.

This truth corrects two opposite errors. Some exalt the Word apart from the Spirit, producing lifeless orthodoxy. Others pursue the Spirit apart from the Word, thereby drifting into emotionalism without anchor.

Jesus never separated them. In John 14:26, He said the Spirit would *"teach you all things and will remind you of everything I have said to you."* The Spirit and the Word operate together - one providing revelation, the other giving language to express it.

The Spirit's role in conviction

The Bible's authority is not merely academic - it is experiential. When the Spirit speaks through the Bible, He pierces the heart, like in Acts 2:37, *"When the people heard this, they were cut to the heart and said to Peter and the other apostles, 'Brothers, what shall we do?'"* This response to Peter's sermon at Pentecost illustrates the Spirit's convicting power through the Word. The same passage that once lay dormant now burns with holy fire.

Conviction is not condemnation. The Spirit never humiliates; He heals. His conviction exposes wounds so that grace may cleanse them. As Hebrews declares, *"The word of God is alive and active. Sharper than any double-edged sword, it penetrates even to dividing soul and spirit, joints and marrow."* (Hebrews 4:12). The Spirit wields Scripture like a surgeon's scalpel - cutting to heal, wounding to restore.

This convicting work distinguishes the Bible from every other book. Literature may inspire, philosophy may challenge, but only Scripture, breathed by the Spirit, transforms. Each time the Word is opened, the Spirit stands ready to confront falsehood, comfort the broken, and conform believers to Christ's likeness. Conviction becomes the sign that the Spirit has spoken, for He always leads us back to repentance and renewal.

The Spirit and the formation of faith

Faith is not generated by human effort; it is birthed by divine revelation. Paul wrote, *"Faith comes from hearing the message, and the message is heard through the word about Christ."* (Romans 10:17). But hearing requires the Spirit's work within. Without Him, the gospel remains information; with Him, it becomes invitation. The Spirit takes the Word and plants it deep within, producing the fruit of faith that no argument could manufacture.

The formation of faith is therefore both rational and relational. The Word provides truth; the Spirit ignites trust. Together they move the heart from belief about God to belief in God. This dynamic explains the explosive growth of the early church.

The same Scriptures the Pharisees had studied for centuries suddenly came alive through the Spirit at Pentecost. The difference was not content but presence - the Word was now accompanied by the wind of divine power.

The Spirit continues this miracle in every generation. Each conversion is a personal Pentecost in miniature - the Word proclaimed, the Spirit applied, the heart transformed. Faith is not inherited or manufactured; it is breathed into being. The Spirit ensures that Scripture is never just read but received, never just studied but believed.

The Spirit and the revelation of Christ

The Holy Spirit's ultimate purpose in Scripture is not to impress us with divine mysteries but to reveal Jesus Christ. From Genesis to Revelation, the Bible's central theme is the Son of God. The Spirit's task is to unveil Him to the heart. In John 15:26, Jesus told His disciples, *"When the Advocate comes, he will testify about me."* The Spirit opens the pages of Scripture so that believers may encounter not just doctrines but a Person.

Every verse, story, and prophecy finds fulfilment in Christ. The Spirit highlights this continuity across the covenants. On the road to Emmaus, the resurrected Jesus explained, *"Beginning with Moses and all the Prophets, he explained to them what was said in all the Scriptures concerning himself."* (Luke 24:27). The disciples later testified, *"Were not our hearts burning within us while he talked with us on the road and opened the Scriptures to us?"* (Luke 24:32). That burning of the heart is the mark of the Spirit's illumination.

The Spirit never draws attention to Himself apart from Christ. His ministry is to make Jesus vivid and central. Whenever the Bible is read with His help, Christ steps off the page into the reader's life.

The Spirit transforms Scripture from information about God into revelation of God. The result is worship - hearts moved to adore the One who was once only admired. Through the Spirit, the Bible becomes a living window through which believers behold the glory of Christ.

The Spirit's presence in the community of faith

The Spirit does not only speak through Scripture to individuals but also within the gathered church. *"Let the message of Christ dwell among you richly as you teach and admonish one another with all wisdom."* (Colossians 3:16). When believers share insights from the Word, pray the Word, or sing the Word, the Spirit orchestrates harmony among them. The same breath that inspired the text breathes unity into its interpreters.

This communal aspect guards against private distortion. No one person holds exclusive insight into God's revelation. The Spirit distributes understanding across the Body, ensuring that the whole church learns together. *"To each one the manifestation of the Spirit is given for the common good."* (1 Corinthians 12:7). When believers gather around Scripture with humility, the Spirit weaves their insights into a fuller picture of truth.

In this way, the Spirit maintains both diversity and unity. He allows for different emphases and applications while preserving doctrinal harmony. The church, filled with the Spirit, becomes the living commentary on the Bible. Its collective witness across centuries demonstrates that the same Spirit who inspired the apostles still interprets their words in every age. The Spirit in the Word and the Spirit in the church are not two voices but one.

The Spirit's role in memory and guidance

The Spirit not only reveals truth but helps believers remember and apply it. In John 14:26, Jesus promised, *"The Holy Spirit... will teach you all things and will remind you of everything I have said to you."* This ministry of remembrance ensures that Scripture is not confined to the page but carried in the heart. The Spirit brings forgotten verses to mind at the exact moment they are needed, proving that God's Word never returns empty.

This guidance is deeply personal. In moments of decision or distress, the Spirit draws from the reservoir of Scripture within us, providing timely wisdom. A single verse, long buried in memory, can become the lifeline of faith. The Spirit's role is not merely to teach but to time - to bring the right truth to light in the right season. *"The Sovereign Lord has given me a well-instructed tongue, to know the word that sustains the weary."* (Isaiah 50:4). For this reason, believers must store up the Word. The Spirit cannot remind us of what we have never read. The more Scripture we internalise, the more material He can use to guide and comfort us. The Word in our minds becomes the vocabulary of the Spirit in our hearts. Through this divine partnership, the Bible becomes not just a record of revelation but a companion of daily direction.

The Spirit and the Unity of the Testaments

Another work of the Spirit is to reveal the coherence between the Old and New Testaments. Without Him, the Bible can appear fragmented - aw against grace, judgment against mercy. But the Spirit reveals a single story of redemption unfolding through history, as we see in Revelation 19:10, *"The testimony of Jesus is the spirit of prophecy."* The same Spirit who spoke through the prophets now interprets their message in the light of Christ.

Through His illumination, believers see that the Old Testament anticipates the New, and the New fulfils the Old. The promises, patterns, and prophecies of the ancient Scriptures all find their meaning in Jesus. The Spirit connects what time separated. He enables readers to trace the crimson thread of grace running from Eden's promise to Calvary's cross. Without His insight, Scripture remains a library of disconnected books; with Him, it becomes a symphony of divine purpose.

This unity also affirms the Spirit's authorship. Only a single divine Mind could inspire such coherence across centuries, languages, and cultures. The Spirit's consistency throughout Scripture confirms that the Bible is not a collection of human reflections about God but God's own revelation of Himself through human voices. The unity of the two Testaments is the fingerprint of the Holy Spirit.

The Spirit and the reader's transformation

The Spirit's ultimate goal in Scripture is transformation, not mere information. *"We all, who with unveiled faces contemplate the Lord's glory, are being transformed into his image with ever-increasing glory, which comes from the Lord, who is the Spirit."* (2 Corinthians 3:18). The Bible becomes a mirror in which believers see both who they are and who they are becoming in Christ.

The Spirit does not simply interpret the Word; He incarnates it in the reader's life. Every truth revealed demands a response. The Spirit takes doctrine and turns it into devotion, turning knowledge into obedience. As believers yield, the Word becomes flesh again - not in the sense of incarnation, but in embodiment. The life of Jesus begins to shape their attitudes, choices, and relationships. This is the miracle of sanctification through Scripture.

Transformation proves the authenticity of revelation. Those who truly hear the Spirit through the Bible cannot remain unchanged. The same breath that inspired prophets now breathes holiness into God's people. The more the Word fills us, the more the Spirit forms Christ within us. In this union of Word and Spirit, God speaks not only to us but through us, making every believer a living letter of His truth. As Paul expressed so well, *"You show that you are a letter from Christ... written not with ink but with the Spirit of the living God."* (2 Corinthians 3:3)

Inspiration and illumination

The distinction between the Spirit's work in inspiration and illumination is crucial to understanding how the Bible functions. Inspiration refers to the Spirit's past work in producing Scripture; illumination refers to His present work in explaining it. The first ensures the Bible is divine in origin; the second ensures it is divine in effect. Without inspiration, the Bible would be human opinion; without illumination, it would remain a sealed mystery. The Spirit who breathed out the text continues to breathe life into it. The Psalmist prayed, *"Open my eyes that I may see wonderful things in your law."* (Psalm 119:18)

This is illumination - the Spirit granting spiritual perception to comprehend divine truth. It is not new revelation but new understanding of existing revelation. The same words are read, yet their meaning penetrates deeper because the Spirit has opened the heart.

The unspiritual mind can try to analyse Scripture, but it cannot apprehend its power. Paul said, *"The person without the Spirit does not accept the things that come from the Spirit of God but considers them foolishness and cannot understand them because they are discerned only through the Spirit."* (1 Corinthians 2:14). Academic knowledge can describe what the Bible says, but only the Spirit can reveal what it means. Inspiration will guarantee accuracy; illumination will grant intimacy. The Holy Spirit does both.

The Spirit's Partnership with the Word

The Word of God and the Spirit of God will never work independently. Wherever the Spirit moves, He carries the Word; wherever the Word is proclaimed, the Spirit empowers it. This divine partnership has been evident since creation. *"Now the earth was formless and empty, darkness was over the surface of the deep, and the Spirit of God was hovering over the waters. And God said, 'Let there be light.'"* (Genesis 1:2-3). The Word was spoken, and the Spirit activated it. Together they brought order from chaos, light from darkness, and life from emptiness.

The same miracle occurs spiritually whenever Scripture is read or preached in the Spirit's power. The Word provides form; the Spirit provides force. The Word declares truth; the Spirit drives it into hearts. This is why preaching without the Spirit becomes lifeless, and spirituality without the Word becomes lawless. The church stands strong only when both are honoured.

Jesus demonstrated this union in His ministry. Every time He quoted Scripture, He did so under the Spirit's anointing. When Jesus was tempted in the wilderness, He simply declared, *"It is written…"* (Matthew 4:4). The written Word became the living weapon by the Spirit's power. Likewise, the Spirit always brings believers back to the Word as the measure of truth.

Any supposed "move of the Spirit" that disregards Scripture cannot be of Him, for He is the Spirit of truth. *"He will not speak on his own; he will speak only what he hears."* (John 16:13)

The Spirit's power in preaching

Throughout history, revival has always occurred where the Spirit and the Word converge. The early apostles experienced this at Pentecost. Peter's sermon was not eloquent rhetoric but Spirit-empowered proclamation. *"When they heard this, they were cut to the heart."* (Acts 2:37). The same words of Scripture that others had heard countless times suddenly carried divine conviction. The Spirit turned information into transformation.

Preaching empowered by the Spirit transcends human ability. The preacher becomes a vessel rather than a performer. The difference is not volume or style but unction - the tangible awareness that the words being spoken are alive. *"My message and my preaching were not with wise and persuasive words, but with a demonstration of the Spirit's power."* (1 Corinthians 2:4). The Spirit gives voice to the Word, awakening repentance and faith in the listener.

Without the Spirit, preaching becomes mere explanation; with the Spirit, it becomes revelation. A sermon may be well-crafted and accurate yet still barren if not accompanied by divine breath. Conversely, a simple word spoken under anointing can pierce the hardest heart. As the Apostle Paul said, the Spirit honours the preached Word because it bears the fragrance of Christ. *"For we are to God the pleasing aroma of Christ among those who are being saved."* (2 Corinthians 2:15)

The Spirit and the Living Word

The Bible is not an end in itself but a means to encounter the Living Word - Jesus Christ. The Spirit ensures that Scripture never becomes an idol. *"You study the Scriptures diligently because you think that in them you have eternal life. These are the very Scriptures that testify about me."* (John 5:39). The Pharisees knew the text but missed the Person.

The Spirit rescues believers from the same trap by transforming reading into relationship. When the Spirit illuminates Scripture, it ceases to be merely historical record and becomes present revelation. Passages written to ancient Israel suddenly speak directly into today's circumstances. This is not because meaning changes but because the Spirit applies timeless truth to timely need. A verse becomes a voice; a promise becomes power. *"The grass withers and the flowers fall, but the word of our God endures forever."* (Isaiah 40:8)

The Spirit turns study into communion. Reading the Bible in His presence is a two-way conversation. We read the Word, and the Word reads us. The Spirit makes this exchange possible, convicting, comforting, and commissioning as needed. Scripture under His touch becomes not just something to interpret but something to experience. Through Him, the written Word reveals the Living Word, and believers find themselves face to face with Christ.

The Spirit and the renewal of the mind

The Spirit's illumination does more than increase knowledge - it renews perception. Paul urged believers in Romans 12:2, *"Do not conform to the pattern of this world, but be transformed by the renewing of your mind."* The Holy Spirit uses Scripture as His instrument to reshape our thinking into alignment with God's truth. Every lie we have believed is displaced by light from the Word.

This renewal is both instantaneous and ongoing. At conversion, the Spirit opens our understanding to the gospel. Thereafter, He continually refines it, aligning our thoughts with the mind of Christ. *"We have the mind of Christ."* (1 Corinthians 2:16). The Bible provides the blueprint; the Spirit supplies the building power. Together they reconstruct our worldview from the inside out.

Renewal by the Word and Spirit affects everything - emotions, ethics, and everyday choices. The believer begins to see as God sees, value what He values, and desire what He desires.

This transformation proves that hearing Scripture through the Spirit is not about gaining insight but about gaining likeness to Christ. Every revelation becomes a renovation. The Spirit turns Bible study into sanctification, shaping hearts into living testimonies of grace.

The Spirit and the sanctifying Word

The Holy Spirit not only reveals truth but also uses truth to purify the believer. Jesus prayed for His disciples, *"Sanctify them by the truth; your word is truth."* (John 17:17). Sanctification is the Spirit's ongoing work of shaping our inner life to reflect Christ's character, and Scripture is His chosen instrument. Every command, promise, and principle becomes material for transformation as the Spirit applies it to the heart. Sanctification by the Word is not achieved by willpower but by willingness. The Spirit does not impose holiness; He invites surrender.

As believers yield to the Word's authority, the Spirit begins to remove the residue of the old life. He convicts of sin, comforts in repentance, and strengthens in obedience. This process can be painful, for God's Word exposes what must die before new life can flourish. *"Is not my word like fire,"* declares the Lord, *"and like a hammer that breaks a rock in pieces?"* (Jeremiah 23:29)

The Spirit wields the Word as both scalpel and seed - cutting what is diseased and planting what is divine. The result is the fruitfulness Paul describes so well: *"The fruit of the Spirit is love, joy, peace, forbearance, kindness, goodness, faithfulness, gentleness and self-control."* (Galatians 5:22–23) The Spirit grows this fruit from the soil of Scripture. Each time we obey the Word, we yield more space for His sanctifying presence.

The Spirit's voice in the Bible's boundaries

One of the profound evidences of the Spirit's sovereignty is the formation of the biblical canon itself - the collection of books recognised as Scripture. The same Spirit who inspired the authors also guided the church in recognising their authority. Human councils did not *create* the canon; they confirmed what the Spirit had already made clear.

Jesus promised, *"When he, the Spirit of truth, comes, he will guide you into all the truth."* (John 16:13) That promise extends not only to personal illumination but to the corporate discernment of the church. This means the boundaries of Scripture are Spirit-defined. What some regard as historical coincidence was in fact divine orchestration. Books that lacked the Spirit's unmistakable signature gradually fell away; those that bore His breath endured.

The Spirit inspired not only what was included but also what was excluded. The same divine hand that breathed words into being also determined which words would remain for those who would read and study them through time.

The canon's completeness guards believers from error. When the Spirit speaks today, He does so in continuity with what He has already said. There are no "lost books" waiting to expand revelation, no hidden knowledge outside the Word of God. The Spirit may illuminate endlessly, but He will never innovate beyond the truth of Scripture. The closed canon is not the silence of God - it is the stability of His truth.

The Spirit and the global Word

The Holy Spirit transcends language, culture, and geography, carrying the Word of God into every corner of the earth. We see in Acts 2:6, at Pentecost, believers heard the gospel in their own tongues. *"Each one heard their own language being spoken."* That moment was not only linguistic but prophetic - the Spirit would ensure that the Word could be understood by all peoples.

The translation and transmission of Scripture through history bear witness to this ongoing mission. From the Septuagint to modern versions in thousands of languages, the Spirit has preserved meaning while adapting medium. Each translation is more than scholarship; it is stewardship of revelation. The same Spirit who inspired the Hebrew poet and Greek evangelist now speaks through translators, missionaries, and digital media, ensuring the Word reaches every tribe and tongue.

This global movement of the Spirit also humbles the church. No single culture possesses a monopoly on divine understanding. The Spirit speaks with a multitude of accents, yet always with one voice. Each culture brings fresh perspective to the Word's inexhaustible depth.

The global church becomes a choir in which every language adds harmony to the same song of redemption. *"After this I looked, and there before me was a great multitude that no one could count, from every nation, tribe, people and language, standing before the throne and before the Lamb.* (Revelation 7:9)

The Spirit and the Word in mission

The Spirit's partnership with the Word extends beyond the believer's life into the church's witness. Every genuine movement of evangelism is born from this union. The apostles prayed, *"Now, Lord, consider their threats and enable your servants to speak your word with great boldness."* (Acts 4:29) The Spirit answered with power, shaking the place where they prayed and filling them with courage. The gospel advanced not by strategy but by Spirit-filled speech.

Mission without the Word lacks foundation; the Word without the Spirit lacks fire. When both converge, nations change. The Spirit ignites passion for Scripture and gives utterance that transcends intellect. A single verse spoken under His prompting can pierce hearts across cultures. The Spirit who inspired the Word now impels its proclamation. He sends believers into the world as living echoes of the divine voice. *"You will receive power when the Holy Spirit comes on you; and you will be my witnesses."* (Acts 1:8)

The church's mission, therefore, is not to invent new messages but to carry the old one with fresh anointing. The Spirit empowers ordinary people to speak extraordinary truth. Wherever the Word goes forth in dependence on Him, miracles of faith follow. The Spirit does not compete with the Word; He completes it - turning Scripture into living testimony.

The Spirit who brings it all together

In the final analysis, the Bible and the Holy Spirit are inseparable expressions of one divine intention - to reveal the heart of God and restore relationship with His people. The Spirit inspired the Word, preserves it, interprets it, and applies it. Through Him, the Scriptures remain ever ancient and ever new. The believer who reads with the Spirit reads with the Author Himself as teacher and guide.

When Word and Spirit unite, revival always follows. History confirms it: every awakening has begun when Scripture was rediscovered under the breath of the Spirit. Together they bring revelation and renewal, authority and intimacy, truth and power. The Spirit makes the Word not merely a message about life but the very means by which life flows. *"The words I have spoken to you - they are full of the Spirit and life."* (John 6:63)

This sacred partnership invites continual dependence. To read the Bible without the Spirit is to handle fire without flame; to pursue the Spirit without the Bible is to follow wind without direction. The two together form the heart of Christian experience - the breath and the book, the wind and the Word, the voice and the vessel. Through them, God still speaks today with undiminished power and unfailing love.

The Spirit who writes on the heart

From the beginning, God's desire has been not only to give His Word but to inscribe it within His people. Under the old covenant, His commands were written on stone tablets; under the new Covenant, they are written on living hearts. *"This is the covenant I will make with the people of Israel after that time,"* declares the Lord. *"I will put my law in their minds and write it on their hearts."* (Jeremiah 31:33) The Holy Spirit is the divine pen who performs this inner inscription.

Paul described believers as *"a letter from Christ... written not with ink but with the Spirit of the living God."* (2 Corinthians 3:3). The Spirit turns the external Word into internal witness.

What was once command becomes character, what was once instruction becomes instinct. Through this miracle of inward writing, Scripture moves from the page to the person. The believer becomes living evidence of the Word's truth, a walking testimony of divine authorship.

This transformation distinguishes biblical faith from all other religions. Other systems impose rules; the Spirit imparts renewal. He engraves God's will into the conscience so that obedience becomes not forced but natural. The Spirit fulfils what the prophets foresaw - a people empowered to live God's truth from within rather than compelled by law from without. *"I will give you a new heart and put a new spirit in you… and move you to follow my decrees."* (Ezekiel 36:26–27)

The Spirit and the power of remembrance

When the Spirit writes the Word on the heart, He also safeguards it through remembrance. Jesus promised, *"The Holy Spirit… will teach you all things and will remind you of everything I have said to you."* (John 14:26) This ministry of memory is one of the Spirit's most tender works. He recalls truth precisely when it is needed - verses long forgotten, promises buried under pressure, warnings before temptation.

This divine recall is not random but relational. The Spirit draws from the reservoir of Scripture within us, selecting truths suited to our moment. In fear, He reminds us, *"Do not be afraid, for I am with you."* (Isaiah 41:10). In guilt, He whispers, *"There is now no condemnation for those who are in Christ Jesus."* (Romans 8:1). During confusion, He brings to mind, *"Trust in the Lord with all your heart and lean not on your own understanding."* (Proverbs 3:5). The Spirit becomes both librarian and interpreter, cataloguing and conveying God's words to strengthen faith.

For this reason, Scripture memorisation is not mere discipline; it is partnership with the Spirit. The more truth we store, the more the Spirit can supply. Each verse becomes a seed He can awaken at the appointed time. What we hide in our hearts today becomes the Spirit's vocabulary tomorrow.

The believer who treasures the Word equips the Spirit with endless means to comfort, correct, and guide. *"I have hidden your word in my heart that I might not sin against you."*(Psalm 119:11)

The Spirit and the unity of doctrine

The same Spirit who illuminates the individual mind also guards the corporate mind of the church. Throughout history, the Spirit has preserved doctrinal unity amid diversity of cultures and contexts. Jesus promised that the Spirit would *"guide you into all the truth."* (John 16:13) This guidance was not limited to the apostles but continues through the Spirit's ongoing presence in the Body of Christ.

That's why, despite linguistic, geographical, and denominational differences, the core truths of the gospel remain unchanged. The Spirit safeguards essentials - Christ's divinity, His atoning death, His bodily resurrection, salvation by grace through faith, and the authority of Scripture. Human councils may debate language, but the Spirit ensures that truth itself endures. He guards the heart of doctrine even when the vocabulary of doctrine evolves.

This protective ministry does not eliminate the diversity of interpretation but prevents deviation from revelation. The Spirit allows theological variety where Scripture allows it but enforces unity where Scripture defines it. In this way, the church becomes both flexible and firm - diverse in expression yet united in confession. The same Spirit who inspired the Word preserves its meaning across time. *"Your word, Lord, is eternal; it stands firm in the heavens."* (Psalm 119:89)

The Spirit and the purity of interpretation

The Spirit also sanctifies the process of interpretation. Human pride and presumption easily distort the Bible's meaning, but the Spirit humbles the interpreter. He reminds us that understanding Scripture is not a conquest of intellect but a gift of grace. *"He leads the humble in what is right and teaches them his way."* (Psalm 25:9). The proud approach Scripture to master it; the humble approach to be mastered by it. The Spirit teaches only those willing to be taught.

Spiritual pride has produced countless heresies throughout history. When individuals claim private revelation divorced from the Word or the wider Body, they drift from truth. The Spirit never contradicts Himself; therefore, He never contradicts Scripture. True interpretation occurs not in isolation but in communion - with the Spirit and with the church. *"In the multitude of counsellors there is safety."* (Proverbs 11:14)

The Spirit's purity also protects against manipulation. Those who twist Scripture for selfish ends grieve Him deeply. He will not endorse interpretation that inflates ego or oppresses others. The Spirit of truth never serves deceit. He interprets the Bible in harmony with its Author's character - holy love. When the Spirit enlightens, the result is humility, repentance, and worship, never arrogance or control. To read Scripture rightly is to bow before the One who speaks through it.

5. The Spirit and the renewal of worship
When the Holy Spirit breathes through Scripture, worship naturally follows. The Bible becomes not just a great source of knowledge but a spring of adoration. Every revelation of truth calls forth a response of praise. *"The unfolding of your words gives light."* (Psalm 119:130). That light illuminates the glory of God and ignites the heart of the believer. The Spirit transforms Bible reading into worship, study into song.

The Psalms embody this union of Word and worship. They teach theology through doxology. Each truth proclaimed becomes a prayer, each doctrine a declaration of delight. The Spirit still leads believers in this rhythm - revealing God through the Word so that worship becomes inevitable. *"God is spirit, and his worshippers must worship in the Spirit and in truth."* (John 4:24). Truth alone can become cold; Spirit alone can become chaotic; together they become holy fire.

The Spirit also renews corporate worship through Scripture. When congregations read, sing, and pray the Word, the Spirit fills the atmosphere with divine reality. The church therefore encounters God not through emotional intensity but through biblical intimacy.

The same voice that thundered at Sinai now whispers in hearts during worship, reminding believers that the Word is not a relic to be recited but a revelation to be rejoiced in. Where the Spirit and the Word meet, heaven touches earth.

The Spirit and the maturity of the believer

The Spirit not only teaches Scripture; He matures those who live by it. Spiritual growth is not measured by knowledge alone but by obedience, wisdom, and discernment shaped through the Word. *"Solid food is for the mature, who by constant use have trained themselves to distinguish good from evil."* (Hebrews 5:14). The Spirit trains believers through consistent exposure to Scripture until truth becomes instinct.

This maturity cannot be rushed. The Spirit uses seasons of testing to deepen dependence on the Word. Each trial becomes a classroom in which biblical truth is proven trustworthy. *"The rain came down, the streams rose, and the winds blew and beat against that house; yet it did not fall, because it had its foundation on the rock."* (Matthew 7:25). The rock is Christ, revealed through the Word and reinforced by the Spirit.

As believers grow, they move from consuming Scripture to being consumed by it. The Spirit gradually replaces self-reliance with submission, transforming understanding into instinct. Mature Christians no longer ask only, *"What does this verse mean?"* but *"How does this truth live in me?"* The Holy Spirit's goal is not information but incarnation - the Word made flesh again in every disciple. This maturity equips the church to withstand false teaching and reflect God's wisdom in a confused world.

The Spirit and the discipline of listening

Listening to Scripture is an art taught by the Spirit. In a world saturated with noise, the Spirit cultivates inner quiet where God's Word can be heard. The psalmist wrote, *"Be still, and know that I am God."* (Psalm 46:10). Stillness is not passivity but attentiveness - the readiness to receive divine speech. The Spirit enables believers to hear beyond words to the will of God expressed in them.

The discipline of listening involves surrendering the urge to control what Scripture says. Many read the Bible to confirm their opinions rather than confront them. The Spirit reverses this impulse, teaching us to let the Word read us. In silence and humility, the Spirit uncovers motives, challenges assumptions, and softens resistance. Only then does revelation become transformation.

Listening also requires patience. The Spirit rarely shouts; He often whispers. His voice comes through meditation more than haste, reflection more than reaction. *"In repentance and rest is your salvation, in quietness and trust is your strength."* (Isaiah 30:15). The believer who learns to listen discovers that Scripture speaks endlessly to the soul willing to wait. The Spirit rewards stillness with clarity and fills quiet obedience with divine strength.

The Spirit and the Discernment of Voices

In an age of spiritual confusion, discerning the Spirit's voice from countless imitations is essential. The Bible remains the standard against which every claim of revelation must be tested. *"Dear friends, do not believe every spirit, but test the spirits to see whether they are from God."* (1 John 4:1)

The Spirit of truth never contradicts the Word of truth. Any message, dream, or prophecy inconsistent with Scripture's witness cannot originate from Him. The Spirit also grants discernment to recognise tone as well as content. God's voice is consistent with His nature - gentle yet firm, convicting yet compassionate. The enemy manipulates through fear or flattery; the Spirit leads through peace and purpose. *"Let the peace of Christ rule in your hearts."* (Colossians 3:15)

Peace is not the absence of conflict but the presence of alignment with God's will. The Spirit's inner witness and the Bible's outer authority work together to protect believers from deception. True discernment always emerges through intimacy, not merely intellect. The more time spent in Scripture, the more familiar the believer becomes with the Shepherd's voice. Jesus said, *"His sheep follow him because they know his voice."* (John 10:4)

The Holy Spirit cultivates that recognition through continual communion. Discernment, therefore, is not suspicion - it is sensitivity to the One who speaks through the Word with unmistakable authority and love.

The Spirit and the enduring relevance of Scripture

The Bible remains eternally relevant because the Spirit continually re-applies it to new times and contexts. Cultural settings change, but human nature does not, and neither does divine truth. The Spirit bridges centuries, translating eternal principles into present obedience. *"The word of the Lord endures forever."* (1 Peter 1:25). What was written to ancient Israel still speaks to modern disciples because the same Spirit addresses both.

This dynamic relevance protects the church from both nostalgia and novelty. The Spirit prevents Scripture from becoming a museum relic of past revelation or a canvas for modern invention. He preserves the ancient Word's integrity while also unveiling its fresh implications. Each generation hears anew what has never ceased being true. The Spirit ensures that the Bible remains both rooted and radiant - rooted in its original meaning, radiant in its ongoing power.

The Spirit's voice never grows outdated because He speaks from eternity. The same truth that revived hearts in the first century still renews hearts in the twenty-first. The Spirit keeps the Bible young in every age, not by altering its content but by awakening its relevance. Scripture stays alive because the Spirit who inspired it is eternally alive. He makes the ancient Word ever contemporary, the written text ever living.

The Spirit and the final word

The union of the Bible and the Holy Spirit culminates in one ultimate purpose - to glorify Jesus Christ and bring humanity into communion with God. The Spirit inspired the first word of Scripture and will confirm the last. *"The Spirit and the bride say, 'Come!'"* (Revelation 22:17)

From Genesis to Revelation, the Spirit speaks the same invitation - to hear, believe, and come to the living Word. Every time the Spirit illuminates Scripture, He draws believers closer to the Author of both the book and their faith.

The Spirit does not replace the Bible; He realises it in us. Through Him, the Word moves from information to incarnation, from doctrine to devotion, from history to holiness. *"He who has an ear, let him hear what the Spirit says to the churches."* (Revelation 3:22). That summons still echoes today.

When the believer reads with the Spirit, heaven touches the heart. The same voice that called light from darkness now calls faith from unbelief. The Bible is no longer merely a record of what God once said but the revelation of what He is still saying. Through the Spirit, the Word remains alive - ever ancient, ever new, ever true.

7. READING IN CONTEXT

Every heresy in church history and nearly every distortion of truth in modern preaching can be traced to one common source: Scripture taken out of context. The Bible is often quoted, rarely read, and even less often understood in the light in which it was written. Words spoken to Israel are mistaken as promises to modern nations; poetic imagery is treated as doctrine; metaphors are pressed into literalism. When context is ignored, the meaning of Scripture is mangled.

Reading in context means reading *as the text intends*. It honours the circumstances, language, audience, and purpose of the original writing. The Bible did not fall from heaven in English paragraphs — it emerged from centuries of divine revelation within real cultures and events. To read it faithfully, we must step into that world before drawing it into ours. As Paul urged Timothy, *"Do your best to present yourself to God as one approved, a worker who does not need to be ashamed and who correctly handles the word of truth."* (2 Timothy 2:15)

Correctly handling the Word requires humility - the willingness to listen before we speak. We must allow the text to explain itself rather than forcing it to support our preferences. Scripture was not written to justify our opinions but to reveal God's heart. When we treat the Bible as a divine conversation rather than a collection of quotations, we rediscover its power. The Spirit inspired context as much as content, and both are essential to understanding truth.

The danger of isolation

When a verse is separated from its setting, it can be made to say almost anything. Throughout history, this has been the source of spiritual abuse, political manipulation, and much theological confusion. The serpent in Eden was the first to twist God's Word by selective quotation: *"Did God really say, 'You must not eat from any tree in the garden'?"* (Genesis 3:1). The devil knew how to quote - he just chose to ignore context.

Jesus Himself was tempted with Scripture taken out of context. In the wilderness, Satan urged Him to leap from the temple roof, quoting Psalm 91: *"He will command his angels concerning you."* (Matthew 4:6). But Jesus replied with Scripture quotes in context: *"It is also written: 'Do not put the Lord your God to the test.'"* (Matthew 4:7). The Lord's response teaches us that every text must be balanced by the whole counsel of God. The Bible interprets itself when read holistically.

Isolated interpretation often arises from good intentions but leads to dangerous conclusions. The Bible was never meant to be mined for motivational slogans or prooftexts. It is a unified revelation of God's redemptive plan. A single verse detached from its paragraph, chapter, and book loses the melody of Scripture's symphony. As with music, to appreciate the harmony one must hear all the parts together. The Spirit speaks through the whole score, not the scattered notes.

The Bible's many contexts

Reading in context involves multiple layers of understanding. Each passage exists within at least four dimensions of meaning: literary, historical, theological, and canonical. The *literary context* asks what kind of writing this is - poetry, law, prophecy, narrative, or letter - and interprets accordingly. The *historical context* asks when and why it was written, to whom, and under what circumstances. The *theological context* considers how it reveals God's nature and purposes. The *canonical context* views each passage within the grand story of Scripture as a whole.

Take Jeremiah 29:11, for example - *"For I know the plans I have for you, declares the Lord, plans to prosper you and not to harm you."* Quoted in isolation, it becomes a blanket promise of personal success. In context, it is a message to exiles in Babylon, assuring them that God's covenant faithfulness would outlast their captivity. The verse still applies to believers today, but through principle, not prescription. The God who preserved Israel in exile preserves His people through all hardship. Context does not diminish the verse's comfort; it deepens it.

Each level of context reveals a layer of divine wisdom. Literary structure unveils beauty; historical background reveals purpose; theology discloses meaning; and the canon displays coherence. Together, they show that the Bible is not a collection of fragments but a living organism - one story, one Author, one message of redemption. Reading in context is not an academic discipline alone; it is an act of worship that honours the integrity of God's revelation.

The Spirit and contextual reading

The Holy Spirit, who inspired the original contexts, also guides believers to read within them. He bridges the gap between ancient setting and modern situation. While He may illuminate timeless truths, He will never contradict the text's intended meaning.

The Spirit will never bypass context - He brings it to life. *"When he, the Spirit of truth, comes, he will guide you into all the truth."* (John 16:13). His illumination deepens understanding rather than distorting it.

This principle safeguards us from spiritual subjectivism. Some claim that *"the Spirit told me"* something through a verse that clearly contradicts its meaning. But the Spirit who inspired Scripture will never reinterpret it against itself. He does not invent new truths; He unveils existing ones. Illumination is the Spirit's work of making the written Word personally relevant without violating its original intent. The difference between illumination and distortion is fidelity to context.

To read contextually under the Spirit's guidance is to experience both discipline and delight. Discipline, because we must restrain our tendency to make Scripture about us; delight, because we discover how Scripture draws us into God's larger story. The Spirit helps us read with reverence and restraint - hearing the Author's voice before adding our own. In doing so, we encounter not only information but transformation. Context protects revelation so that illumination can flourish.

The context of covenant

To read the Bible faithfully, one must read through the lens of covenant. Every verse finds its meaning within God's unfolding relationship with His people. The Old Testament reveals the covenant promises made to Israel; the New Testament reveals their fulfilment in Christ. Ignoring this covenantal framework leads to confusion and misapplication. As the writer to the Hebrews reminds us, *"In the past God spoke to our ancestors through the prophets at many times and in various ways, but in these last days he has spoken to us by his Son."* (Hebrews 1:1–2)

Each covenant represents a stage in God's redemptive plan, not a contradiction of the previous one. When a passage is read without recognising its covenantal setting, the reader will risk applying temporary commands as eternal laws or missing eternal principles which are hidden within temporary symbols. For instance, dietary restrictions in Leviticus made sense under the Old Covenant as markers of holiness, but under the New Covenant, they point to the purity found in Christ. Context preserves continuity while clarifying change.

Covenantal reading also restores the unity of Scripture. The same God who spoke at Sinai now speaks through His Son. The promises made to Abraham find their fulfilment in the church, not by replacement but by expansion — Gentiles grafted into Israel's promise. When Paul wrote that *"all Scripture is God-breathed and useful for teaching,"* (2 Timothy 3:16) he was referring primarily to the Old Testament. To read it in context is to see Christ shining through every page. Covenant context reveals Christ as the thread that ties all revelation together.

The context of culture

Culture shapes language, and language shapes understanding. The Bible was written within ancient Near Eastern, Jewish, and Greco-Roman worlds - contexts vastly different from our own. Yet within those historical frameworks, God revealed truth that transcends time. The interpreter's role is to bridge those worlds, discovering eternal principles beneath cultural expressions.

This is why Paul's exhortation, *"Greet one another with a holy kiss."* (Romans 16:16) is applied today through warm fellowship and mutual affection, not through literal repetition.

Cultural context guards us from misusing Scripture for agendas foreign to its purpose. Many have wrongly justified oppression, greed, or nationalism by reading their culture into the text rather than reading the text into their culture. The Spirit calls the church not to conform Scripture to the world but to allow Scripture to transform the world. The Bible is timeless truth clothed in timely forms. The task of interpretation is to discern which elements belong to each.

Respecting culture also reveals the incarnational nature of God's revelation. Just as Christ entered human flesh, the Word entered human language. God chose to speak within the limitations of culture without being limited by it. Understanding that truth deepens our appreciation for His humility. When we grasp how the eternal Word became understandable within time, we are moved to worship. Reading the Bible culturally is not an academic exercise - it is an act of reverence toward the God who stooped to speak our language.

The context of canon

Every passage of Scripture belongs to the larger canon - the whole collection of inspired books that together form the Bible. This means that interpretation must always be consistent with the total message of Scripture. No verse stands alone. The church fathers summarised this principle in the phrase *analogia fidei* - *"the analogy of faith."* Scripture interprets Scripture because its Author is one. *"The sum of your word is truth."* (Psalm 119:160)

This canonical context helps guard against distortion. When one text appears difficult or ambiguous, it must be read alongside others that speak more clearly. For example, the letter of James emphasises that *"faith without deeds is dead."*(James 2:26). Paul insists that *"a person is justified by faith apart from the works of the law."* (Romans 3:28). Taken in isolation, these statements seem contradictory; in canonical context, they harmonise perfectly.

Paul addresses how one is saved; James describes what saving faith looks like in action. The Spirit ensures that apparent tension becomes theological depth.

Reading canonically also reminds us that revelation is progressive. Later revelation clarifies and completes earlier revelation without negating it. The New Testament does not discard the Old - it fulfils it. Every page contributes to the symphony of salvation, each movement echoing the same theme: God's relentless pursuit of humanity. The Spirit invites believers to read with panoramic vision - to see every verse as part of a whole that culminates in Christ.

The context of community

Finally, true understanding of Scripture requires the community of faith. The Bible was written for the people of God, not for isolated individuals. Reading in context must therefore include listening to the church past and present. The Spirit who guides personal study also speaks through the collective wisdom of centuries. *"Let the message of Christ dwell among you richly as you teach and admonish one another."* (Colossians 3:16). The plural *"you"* matters; understanding grows in fellowship.

Community context protects against private interpretation that veers into error. No believer, however gifted, possesses the whole truth alone. The same Holy Spirit who inspired the Word unites believers in discernment. When Christians gather to study, discuss, and pray over Scripture, the Holy Spirit refines individual insights into shared conviction. Truth becomes clearer when tested by love and humility in community.

The history of interpretation demonstrates this beautifully. From the early creeds to contemporary discipleship groups, God has used the fellowship of believers to clarify truth and correct error. The church has always been the Spirit's classroom. Reading in context, therefore, is not just a solitary pursuit, it is also a shared pilgrimage. The Word that once formed a nation and then a church still gathers believers today around the same table of truth.

The Word misused

The story of the church is littered with examples of Scripture misused through the neglect of context. Verses once written to comfort the oppressed have been weaponised to control them. Passages proclaiming freedom have been twisted to justify slavery. Texts about stewardship have been contorted into promises of prosperity. When Scripture is lifted out of its historical, literary, and theological setting, the message of grace can be turned into a tool of greed.

This misuse does not only occur in extremes - it happens whenever the Bible is made to serve human agendas. We may quote verses selectively to defend our opinions, to silence others, or to reinforce our preferences. But when the Word of God becomes a prop for our arguments rather than a voice that confronts them, it ceases to function as revelation. *"You nullify the word of God for the sake of your tradition."* (Matthew 15:6). The danger is not that we stop quoting Scripture, but that we quote it without surrendering to it.

The tragedy is that such misuse often masquerades as faithfulness. The Pharisees of Jesus' day knew Scripture by heart yet missed its heart entirely. Jesus declared, *"You study the Scriptures diligently because you think that in them you have eternal life. These are the very Scriptures that testify about me, yet you refuse to come to me to have life."* (John 5:39–40). The ultimate test of interpretation is not cleverness but Christlikeness. Every reading that leads away from love, humility, or truth betrays its context and its Author.

The importance of the big picture

To read contextually is to see the Bible as a unified whole. Each verse, paragraph, and book fits within God's grand narrative of creation, fall, redemption, and restoration. This "meta-context" gives coherence to the details. Without it, interpretation becomes fragmented - like admiring individual brushstrokes without recognising the painting they form. Scripture tells one story: God's plan to reconcile all things to Himself through Christ.

"For God was pleased to have all his fullness dwell in him, and through him to reconcile to himself all things." (Colossians 1:19–20)

Seeing the big picture guards against distortion. A verse about judgment must be read in light of mercy; a verse about obedience in light of grace. The Bible is not a collection of competing voices but a symphony of divine truth. Even apparent contradictions reveal the multifaceted nature of God's wisdom. The Spirit enables believers to discern how the parts harmonise. When Scripture is read this way, its unity becomes both a defence against error and a source of awe.

Contextual reading also reveals how every text ultimately points to Christ. After His resurrection, Jesus taught the disciples on the road to Emmaus, *"Beginning with Moses and all the Prophets, he explained to them what was said in all the Scriptures concerning himself."* (Luke 24:27). The context of every verse, in its deepest sense, is Jesus. The Old Testament anticipates Him; the New Testament announces Him; the Spirit continues to reveal Him. To read without seeing Christ is to miss the centre of context itself.

Context as protection

One of the Spirit's greatest gifts in the church's interpretive tradition is protection through context. Misreading Scripture does not only lead to error - it can lead to destruction. Peter warned, *"Our dear brother Paul also wrote you with the wisdom that God gave him. His letters contain some things that are hard to understand, which ignorant and unstable people distort, as they do the other Scriptures, to their own destruction."* (2 Peter 3:15–16). Context protects the reader from the arrogance of assumption and the danger of distortion.

Contextual reading demands patience. It invites us to slow down, to ask some questions, to consider setting, audience, and purpose. It guards against the instant gratification of 'soundbite spirituality.' The Spirit trains mature readers by cultivating reverent curiosity - listening before leaping to conclusions.

As Proverbs 30:5 tells us, every word of God deserves such care. *"Every word of God is flawless; he is a shield to those who take refuge in him."* To read quickly is to risk misunderstanding; to read carefully is to encounter holiness.

The discipline of context also humbles us. We discover that our first impressions are not always correct and that the Bible often challenges rather than confirms our assumptions. Context is not a cage for Scripture but a compass. It keeps interpretation anchored in reality, while allowing the Spirit to breathe fresh application. Just as a tree draws nourishment from its roots, every verse draws power from the soil in which it was planted. Pull it out, and it withers; read it in context, and it flourishes.

The role of historical awareness

Understanding history transforms how we hear Scripture. When we grasp what was happening in the world of the Bible, the words come alive with colour and clarity. The prophets thunder with greater urgency, the psalms sing with richer emotion, the Gospels sparkle with sharper detail.

History provides the stage on which revelation unfolds. *"The Word became flesh and made his dwelling among us."* (John 1:14). The incarnation anchors the eternal in the temporal, proving that context is always central to the revelation itself.

For example, knowing the oppression of Roman occupation illuminates Jesus' words about loving enemies. Recognising the suffering of persecuted Christians in Asia Minor helps us feel the power of the promise in Revelation 2:10, *"Be faithful, even to the point of death, and I will give you life as your victor's crown."* History turns Scripture from abstract instruction into lived testimony. It reminds us that God's Word speaks not from the clouds but from the dust of real places and real pain.

The Spirit uses history to show continuity between then and now. The same God who delivered Israel from Egypt delivers believers from sin. The same Spirit who empowered the early church empowers the church today.

Contextual reading is therefore not an academic luxury - it is spiritual fidelity. The more we understand the original world of the Bible, the more vividly we see its relevance in ours. Context makes history holy.

The role of language and meaning

The Bible speaks in words chosen with divine precision but conveyed through human language. To read in context, we must pay attention to how those words function. The Spirit inspired Hebrew poetry, Greek rhetoric, and Aramaic conversation - each with its own rhythm, metaphor, and nuance. The same word may carry different shades of meaning depending on where and how it appears. Context is the key that unlocks these subtleties.

For instance, when Jesus says in Matthew 5:14, *"You are the light of the world,"* He is not flattering individual brilliance, he is commissioning corporate witness. The plural "you" refers to His followers, the church as the light-bearing community. Without linguistic context, the verse becomes an affirmation of self; within it, a call to mission. Similarly, understanding that the Greek word *ekklesia* means "assembly" rather than "building" transforms how we conceive of church itself. Language studied in context reveals theology lived in practice.

This does not mean that every Christian must become a scholar of ancient languages, but it does mean that humility and curiosity should guide interpretation. The Spirit honours both. Good translations, sound commentaries, and communal study serve as tools in His hands. God is not threatened by our questions; He invites them. The Spirit uses linguistic insight to deepen devotion, not to inflate pride. When we listen carefully to what the text truly says, we honour both the words and the Word.

The balance of literal and figurative

Another dimension of contextual reading is discerning what is literal and what is figurative. The Bible employs poetry, parable, symbol, and vision. The Spirit inspired not only facts but forms.

Taking every image literally can distort meaning just as surely as taking every command metaphorically can dilute it. The key is to discern the genre, purpose, and setting of each passage.

When Jesus says, *"I am the door,"* in John 10:9, He's not describing a physical object but a spiritual reality - access to God through Him alone. When Revelation depicts Christ with a sword coming from His mouth, it is not a grotesque image but a powerful metaphor for the Word that judges and conquers. Literal truth can be communicated through figurative language. The Spirit uses metaphor not to obscure reality but to reveal dimensions of it that words alone cannot contain.

Balancing literal and figurative meaning protects Scripture from both naïve literalism and cynical scepticism. The Spirit helps believers discern what the author intended and how that intent points to Christ. Faithful interpretation neither over-spiritualises history nor flattens mystery into logic. Contextual reading allows symbolism to sing while ensuring truth remains solid. In this harmony of form and fact, the reader experiences Scripture's depth without distorting its design.

The Spirit as our hermeneutic

Ultimately, context is not just a matter of scholarship - it is a matter of relationship. The Holy Spirit Himself is the believer's truest hermeneutic, the living interpreter who connects past revelation to present experience. He does not replace study but completes it. The Spirit is not a shortcut around context; He is the light that reveals it. As Paul writes, *"The Spirit searches all things, even the deep things of God."* (1 Corinthians 2:10)

Under the Holy Spirit's guidance, contextual reading becomes communion. We are not merely analysing ancient words but encountering the living God who still speaks through them. The Spirit awakens discernment, aligning intellect with intimacy. He teaches us to ask the right questions, to notice what we would overlook, and to submit when understanding gives way to wonder. Contextual reading is therefore not cold exegesis but warm worship - it is theology on its knees.

The Spirit also ensures continuity of understanding across generations. He guards the church from drifting into cultural captivity by continually drawing her back to the original voice of Scripture. Through every age, revival has come when the Spirit restored contextual faithfulness – and the rediscovery of what God *actually* said and meant. When the Spirit opens our eyes to context, He opens our hearts to obedience.

The fruit of contextual reading

Reading the Bible in context produces humility, maturity, and discernment. It reminds us that Scripture is not a weapon to wield but a Word to obey. It transforms proof-texters into disciples who listen. It teaches us to approach every passage with reverence, patience, and dependence on the Spirit. *"Your word is a lamp for my feet, a light on my path."* (Psalm 119:105). That light shines clearly only when it is seen in the setting God intended.

Contextual reading also deepens unity in the church. When believers interpret Scripture with shared awareness of history, covenant, language, and community, disagreements diminish and worship intensifies. The same Spirit who inspired the Word harmonises its interpretation among His people. The result is not uniformity of thought but harmony of faith - diverse voices joining one song of truth.

Finally, reading in context renews love for the Author. The more clearly we see what God has said and why, the more deeply we love the One who said it. Scripture ceases to be a rulebook and becomes a revelation of relationship. The Spirit leads us beyond curiosity to communion, beyond knowledge to adoration. When context and Spirit unite, the Bible becomes again what it has always been: the living Word of the living God, perfectly trustworthy, eternally relevant, and gloriously true.

Context and the character of God

The goal of contextual reading is not merely accuracy but revelation. We read in context so that we might see God as He truly is. When passages are removed from their setting, God's character can be misrepresented.

A verse about judgment without its surrounding mercy can make Him seem cruel; a verse about blessing without its conditions can make Him seem indulgent. Context will help guard the integrity of God's revelation. *"The Lord, the Lord, the compassionate and gracious God, slow to anger, abounding in love and faithfulness."* (Exodus 34:6)

Every text must be read through the lens of God's unchanging nature. The same God who judges sin does so because He is holy; the same God who offers mercy does so because He is love.

When readers interpret isolated verses without regard for God's character revealed throughout Scripture, theology becomes fragmented. Context draws us back to the whole portrait - the God who is consistent, covenantal, and compassionate. The Spirit always interprets Scripture in harmony with the heart of the Author.

Understanding context therefore protects believers from constructing an image of God in their own likeness. The Word invites us to conform to God's truth, not to conform God to ours. To read the Bible faithfully is to let it correct our perception of Him. The Spirit does not merely teach us facts about God; He unveils the face of the Father through the face of Christ. And Christ, the living Word, is the perfect context for every written word.

Context and the commands of Scripture

Many controversies in Christian ethics arise from neglecting context. Commands given to Israel under the Mosaic Covenant are sometimes imposed wholesale upon the church, or conversely, dismissed entirely as obsolete. Contextual reading discerns which instructions were culturally or covenantally specific and which express enduring moral principles.

Paul's reminder in 1 Corinthians 10:11, remains vital: *"These things were written down as warnings for us, on whom the culmination of the ages has come."* The Spirit helps believers see the continuity and progression of revelation.

The moral heart of God's law remains - the call to love God and neighbour - but ceremonial and civil components have found fulfilment in Christ. For example, Sabbath rest, once expressed through a day, now finds its substance in a Person: *"Come to me, all you who are weary and burdened, and I will give you rest."* (Matthew 11:28). The Spirit shows that context does not cancel command; it clarifies its purpose.

When believers read commands contextually, obedience becomes relational rather than ritual. The question shifts from *"What must I do?"* to *"What does this reveal about God's will and character?"* Context transforms rule-keeping into response. It liberates the Christian from legalism without leading into licence. The Spirit illuminates not only the letter but the intent of Scripture, guiding believers to apply timeless truth in timely ways.

Context and the promises of Scripture

Few parts of Scripture are more misused than its promises. Pulled from context, they are turned into slogans for personal success or self-affirmation. Yet every promise of God is rooted in covenant relationship and always aimed at His glory, not our convenience. *"For no matter how many promises God has made, they are 'Yes' in Christ."* (2 Corinthians 1:20). The Spirit-centred reading of promises restores perspective.

Promises reveal God's faithfulness, not our entitlement. When God told Joshua, *"I will never leave you nor forsake you,"*(1:5) it was not a motivational phrase but an assurance of divine presence for a daunting mission. The same principle applies to believers today: God's promises empower obedience, not idleness. Context reminds us that every blessing carries a purpose - to equip, sustain, and glorify God through us.

Misapplied promises breed disillusionment. When people claim words God never spoke to them, disappointment replaces faith. Context rescues hope from distortion. The Spirit teaches us to receive promises as invitations into partnership with God, not as guarantees of comfort.

Faith in context does not demand outcomes; it trusts the One who made the promise. When Scripture is read this way, the believer's confidence matures into worship.

Context and the prophecies of Scripture

Prophecy, more than any other genre, requires careful contextual reading. The prophets spoke into specific historical situations while simultaneously revealing eternal principles. To ignore their immediate audience is to miss half their message; to limit them only to that audience is to miss the rest. Prophecy lives in two dimensions: *then* and *now*. The Spirit enables the church to discern both, as 2 Peter 1:20 tells us clearly: *"Above all, you must understand that no prophecy of Scripture came about by the prophet's own interpretation of things."*

Understanding the original context of prophecy guards against sensationalism. The prophets did not write as fortune-tellers but as covenant messengers calling God's people to repentance. When modern readers chase hidden timelines or secret codes, they risk missing the prophetic call to holiness and justice that remains central. The Spirit restores the proper focus: prophecy is not prediction for curiosity but proclamation for transformation. At the same time, the Spirit ensures that prophecy still speaks to the present. The same Spirit who inspired Isaiah's words about the Suffering Servant continues to reveal Christ through them.

Contextual reading holds both history and fulfilment closely together. It recognises that the prophets addressed their own generation *and* anticipated the Messiah. When read with this balance, prophecy becomes not a puzzle to solve but a window into the heart of God.

Context and the parables of Jesus

The parables of Jesus demonstrate the necessity of context perhaps more clearly than any other part of Scripture. These brief, but vivid stories have been cherished, quoted, and misinterpreted in equal measure. Each parable was spoken to a specific audience with a particular purpose, often in response to a question, challenge, or misunderstanding.

To strip a parable from its setting is to lose its sharp edge and its intended shock. *"The disciples came to him and asked, 'Why do you speak to the people in parables?' He replied, 'Because the knowledge of the secrets of the kingdom of heaven has been given to you, but not to them.'"* (Matthew 13:10–11)

Parables are not moral fables but kingdom revelations. They are meant to awaken rather than to entertain. For example, the parable of the prodigal son in Luke 15 is often read as a story about personal repentance, but in context, it is really addressed to Pharisees who resented God's mercy toward sinners. The true sting lies in the elder brother's pride. Similarly, the parable of the Good Samaritan is not merely a call to kindness but a rebuke to legalistic boundaries that exclude compassion. When read in context, parables move from sentiment to confrontation.

The Spirit helps readers hear the parables as the original listeners did - surprised, unsettled, and invited to respond. He reveals their timeless relevance without detaching them from their original challenge. Contextual reading allows the parables to retain their prophetic force, cutting through complacency to expose the heart. The same Spirit who inspired their telling now inspires our hearing, ensuring that their meaning remains alive and piercing.

Context and the Psalms

The Psalms also demand contextual sensitivity. They express the full range of human emotion before God - joy, grief, anger, fear, and hope - but they are not random expressions of mood. Each psalm arises from specific circumstances: a battle fought, a sin confessed, a deliverance remembered. If we are careful to see that background, our worship will be enriched. *"I cried out to the Lord, and he answered me from his holy mountain."* (Psalm 3:4). Understanding that this was written while David fled from Absalom gives depth to his trust amid betrayal.

Reading psalms in context also prevents misapplication. When we encounter imprecatory psalms - those calling for judgment on enemies - we must read them through the lens of the cross.

Christ has borne God's judgment; therefore, believers now pray for redemption rather than retribution. Context transforms vengeance into victory through grace. The Spirit helps us sing these ancient songs with renewed meaning, applying their truth to our era without distorting their heart.

Moreover, the psalms provide a model for contextual prayer. They teach believers how to bring their emotions honestly to God while anchoring them in His character. The psalmists never ignore their circumstances; they interpret them in the light of God's covenant faithfulness. This is contextual reading turned into worship - truth applied through trust. As we read the psalms with the same Spirit who inspired them, lament becomes faith, and fear becomes praise.

Context and contemporary application

The ultimate aim of contextual reading is faithful application. We do not study the Bible merely to understand the past but to live the truth in the present. The challenge lies in discerning what transfers directly and what transfers through principle. The Spirit enables this discernment. He reveals how eternal truth meets temporal reality. *"Everything that was written in the past was written to teach us, so that through the endurance taught in the Scriptures and the encouragement they provide we might have hope."* (Romans 15:4)

Faithful application begins by honouring original intention. We ask, *"What did this mean then?"* before asking, *"What does this mean now?"* The Spirit bridges that gap, translating ancient instruction into contemporary obedience. He applies truth not by changing its meaning but by connecting its message. The believer who reads in context is never left with mere knowledge; he or she is compelled to act. Scripture is not given for speculation but for transformation.

The Spirit's contextual application also protects the church from cultural captivity. Each generation faces the temptation to twist the Word to suit modern sensibilities or social trends. Context reminds us that truth does not evolve with opinion.

God's Word is living because it is eternal, not because it is flexible. The same Spirit who once addressed Israel and the early church still addresses us - but on His terms, not ours. To read in context is to submit our culture to Scripture, not Scripture to culture.

Context and the centrality of Christ

All contextual reading ultimately converges on Christ. He is the living context in which every passage finds meaning. Jesus declared John 5:39, *"These are the very Scriptures that testify about me."* The Law reveals our need for Him; the Prophets announce His coming; the Gospels reveal His glory; the Epistles explain His work; and Revelation unveils His triumph. To read the Bible apart from Christ is to read it out of context.

The Spirit's mission in interpretation is to magnify Christ. He leads believers through the corridors of Scripture until every door opens onto the Saviour. Christ is the thread that ties Genesis to Revelation, creation to consummation, promise to fulfilment. The Bible is not a manual for moral living but a revelation of the Messiah who gives life. When we read every passage with Christ at the centre, context becomes worship and theology becomes doxology.

In the end, reading in context is not simply about method - it is about relationship. We read the Bible not to master it but to be mastered by the One who speaks through it. The Spirit makes context a place of encounter, where the written Word and the living Word meet.

To read in context, therefore, is to read in communion - with the Spirit as our guide, Christ as our focus, and the Father as our goal. *"Then he opened their minds so they could understand the Scriptures."* (Luke 24:45)

The Bible's greatest danger

The Bible's greatest danger has never been neglect - it has always been misuse. From the serpent's first half-truth in Eden to modern pulpits and podcasts, Scripture has been distorted to justify sin, build empires, and silence truth. The enemy rarely attacks the Bible by denying it outright; he attacks by twisting it. As Paul warned, *"Such people are false apostles, deceitful workers, masquerading as apostles of Christ. And no wonder, for Satan himself masquerades as an angel of light."* (2 Corinthians 11:13–14)

The danger of misuse lies not in the text but in the heart that wields it. The same Word that brings life when handled with humility becomes a weapon of destruction when wielded with pride. History is filled with examples - wars fought under the banner of Scripture, slavery defended by selective verses, and manipulation disguised as revelation. The Bible's authority has been exploited to justify actions the Author would never approve. Misuse is not a failure of revelation; it is a failure of reverence.

The tragedy is that every distortion begins with a partial truth. The most dangerous lies are those wrapped in the language of Scripture. That is why the temptation of Jesus' in the wilderness remains the definitive example of how the Word can be misused and how it must be defended. The devil quoted Psalm 91; Jesus quoted Deuteronomy in reply. Jesus defeated deception not by rejecting Scripture but by restoring its context. *"It is written: 'Worship the Lord your God and serve him only.'"* (Luke 4:8). Misuse dies where obedience begins.

The subtlety of distortion

Misuse rarely begins with open rebellion. It starts with subtle shifts - small enough to go unnoticed, significant enough to alter truth. A word emphasised differently, a verse isolated from its paragraph, a doctrine built on a single phrase - these are the beginnings of distortion.

False teaching does not need to reject the Bible; it only needs to rearrange it. As Peter warned, *"They distort the Scriptures, as they do the other writings, to their own destruction."* (2 Peter 3:16)

Distortion often arises when readers seek support for their opinions rather than surrender to God's authority. The Bible becomes a mirror for self-justification instead of a window into divine revelation. When Scripture is used to win arguments instead of to form disciples, its purpose is lost. Every misuse begins with the question, *"What do I want this to mean?"* rather than, *"What did God mean when He said this?"*

The Spirit exposes this subtlety by drawing attention back to the Author's intent. The Word must interpret the reader, not the reader the Word. Hebrews 4:12 declares, *"The word of God is alive and active... it judges the thoughts and attitudes of the heart."*

The Spirit uses Scripture to diagnose motives as well as to reveal truth. Distortion thrives in self-deception; discernment begins in surrender. The moment we stop listening, the text becomes a tool in our hands rather than a voice in our ears.

The misuse of authority

Throughout history, misuse of Scripture has often been linked to misuse of authority. When religious leaders place themselves above the Word, they inevitably twist it to protect their power. Jesus confronted this in His day, saying, *"You have a fine way of setting aside the commands of God in order to observe your own traditions."* (Mark 7:9). Tradition became the tool through which human authority eclipsed divine revelation.

The same danger persists today. Whether in institutions or individuals, whenever interpretation becomes a means of control rather than an act of service, the Spirit is grieved. The Bible is not an instrument of dominance, it is an instrument of liberation. Jesus declared, *"You will know the truth, and the truth will set you free."* (John 8:32). Any teaching that enslaves through fear, guilt, or manipulation betrays the gospel it claims to proclaim.

The Spirit's role is to dethrone the interpreter and enthrone the Word. True authority in the church flows not from position or persuasion but from submission to Scripture. The preacher, teacher, or theologian who kneels before the text stands tall before the world. Those who exalt themselves over it fall under its judgment. As James reminds us, *"Not many of you should become teachers... because you know that we who teach will be judged more strictly."* (James 3:1) Spiritual authority is proven by fidelity, not charisma.

The misuse of emotion

Emotional misuse of Scripture is another form of distortion. In an age that prizes feelings above faith, many approach the Bible as a source of inspiration rather than instruction. Verses are quoted for comfort but ignored for conviction. The psalms of lament are neglected; the promises of prosperity are amplified. The Bible becomes a mood enhancer rather than a mirror of truth. *"For the time will come when people will not put up with sound doctrine. Instead, to suit their own desires, they will gather around them a great number of teachers to say what their itching ears want to hear."* (2 Timothy 4:3)

Emotion is not the enemy - God created it - but it must never govern Bible interpretation. The Spirit uses Scripture to shape emotion, not the other way around. True comfort comes not from selective reading but from surrender to the whole counsel of God. The same Word that wounds also heals; the same truth that convicts also consoles. Spiritual maturity learns to receive both. Misuse arises when we demand that Scripture make us feel better rather than make us more holy.

The Holy Spirit restores balance by transforming emotion into encounter. He allows Scripture to move the heart without manipulating it. The psalms teach us to weep honestly before God; the Gospels teach us to trust even when we cannot see. The emotional life of faith is healthiest when rooted in the objective truth of the Word. The Bible does not conform to our feelings - it re-forms them in light of divine reality. *"Your statutes are my delight; they are my counsellors."* (Psalm 119:24)

The misuse of silence

Another subtle form of distortion comes not from what is said, but from what is *left unsaid*. Some truths are neglected because they are inconvenient or uncomfortable. Preachers may avoid verses that challenge popular opinion or confront sin. Churches may emphasise grace while ignoring holiness, or justice without mercy. Yet omission can distort the gospel just as much as exaggeration. Paul declared to the Ephesian elders, *"I have not hesitated to proclaim to you the whole will of God."* (Acts 20:27)

Partial truth is often more dangerous than outright error because it appears orthodox. When Scripture is selectively preached or partially believed, the message becomes unbalanced. Grace without repentance becomes indulgence; holiness without grace becomes condemnation. The Spirit inspired every word for a reason. To neglect any part of God's Word is to diminish its power. *"All Scripture is God-breathed and is useful for teaching, rebuking, correcting and training in righteousness."* (2 Timothy 3:16). The Spirit does not edit revelation to make it palatable; He empowers believers to receive it in full.

Faithfulness to Scripture requires courage - to speak when it is unpopular and to stay silent when speculation would only confuse. The Spirit leads preachers and teachers to discern when to emphasise, when to explain, and when to simply stand in awe. Silence is holy when it flows from reverence, but sinful when it hides the truth. Misuse begins when human comfort takes precedence over divine command. The Word was never meant to be managed; it was meant to be proclaimed.

The misuse of mystery

Closely related to silence is the misuse of mystery. Some elevate mystery above revelation, claiming spiritual superiority by insisting that truth cannot be known. Others deny mystery altogether, demanding certainty where God has left room for faith. Both errors distort the Bible's purpose. The Spirit gives revelation, but not complete explanation. *"The secret things belong to the Lord our God, but the things revealed belong to us and to our children forever."* (Deuteronomy 29:29)

Healthy theology embraces mystery without manufacturing it. It accepts the limits of human understanding while rejoicing in what has been clearly revealed. Misuse occurs when mystery becomes a cloak for false teaching or when revelation is forced to answer questions it was never meant to address. The Spirit does not satisfy curiosity; He sanctifies it. He draws believers to wonder rather than wander. Faith thrives not on the absence of questions but on trust in the One who holds the answers.

The balance between revelation and mystery protects the believer from arrogance. It reminds us that knowledge is a gift, not a weapon. Paul's warning still stands: *"Knowledge puffs up, but love builds up."* (1 Corinthians 8:1). The Spirit ensures that revelation leads to reverence, not rivalry. When Scripture is read with this humility, mystery then becomes worship rather than confusion and understanding becomes gratitude rather than pride.

The misuse of words

Sometimes Scripture is misused not by what it teaches, but by how its words are handled. Words can be lifted, twisted, or redefined to suit agendas. Cults and ideologies thrive on rewording biblical terms while retaining their familiarity. "Sin" becomes "mistake"; "repentance" becomes "personal growth"; "salvation" becomes "self-fulfilment." The vocabulary of truth is retained, but its meaning is subtly reversed. This is precisely how deception will grow undetected. *"Woe to those who call evil good and good evil, who put darkness for light and light for darkness."* (Isaiah 5:20)

Language is sacred because it shapes understanding. God revealed Himself in words, and the Spirit preserves those words to convey meaning faithfully. When words are emptied of their biblical weight, theology collapses into sentiment. The Spirit safeguards truth by anchoring meaning in revelation, not redefinition. He teaches believers to discern when familiar phrases hide foreign ideas. As John exhorts, *"Let what you heard from the beginning remain in you."* (1 John 2:24). Misuse begins when language loses its link to the Lord.

Faithful interpretation therefore requires linguistic vigilance. The church must guard not only what Scripture says but what it means. The Spirit ensures that words remain windows into truth rather than walls that conceal it. When language is purified by the Spirit's guidance, communication becomes communion - the words of God carrying the presence of God to the hearts of His people.

The path back to integrity

The antidote to misuse and misunderstanding is not suspicion but submission. The remedy for distortion is devotion. Scripture cannot be rightly handled by those who wish to master it; it can only be understood by those willing to be mastered by it. *"The fear of the Lord is the beginning of wisdom."* (Proverbs 9:10)

Reverence restores perspective. The Spirit calls believers back to humility - to approach the Bible not as critics dissecting a text but as children listening to their Father.

Integrity in interpretation is a lifelong pursuit. It involves continual repentance for the times we have read carelessly or selfishly. It requires community, accountability, and dependence on the Spirit. Misuse flourishes in isolation; understanding grows in fellowship. As believers gather around the Word with open hearts and discerning minds, the Spirit rebuilds trust where confusion once reigned. Truth reclaims its place, and the church rediscovers its voice.

Above all, integrity in Scripture leads to intimacy with Christ. The Spirit never restores the Word to prominence without also restoring the Word made flesh to pre-eminence. Jesus is the measure of every interpretation and the mirror of every application. When He is central, misuse withers.

The Spirit who inspired the Word defends it still - not through argument but through transformation. When hearts are yielded, truth is protected, and the Word once misused becomes the Word once again proclaimed in power.

Misunderstanding as a matter of the heart

Misunderstanding the Bible is not always the result of ignorance; often, it stems from wilful resistance. The greatest obstacle to understanding is not intellectual limitation but spiritual pride. The Pharisees of Jesus' day were experts in Scripture yet blind to its fulfilment standing before them. *"You know neither the Scriptures nor the power of God."* (Mark 12:24). Their problem was not that they didn't read - it was that they didn't listen.

True understanding begins in humility. The Spirit reveals truth to those who come as learners, not masters. *"He guides the humble in what is right and teaches them his way."* (Psalm 25:9). The mind that insists on being right will always misread revelation, because the Bible's purpose is not to gratify curiosity but to produce obedience. The Spirit resists the proud but opens Scripture to the contrite. This is why Jesus could say, *"I praise you, Father... because you have hidden these things from the wise and learned and revealed them to little children."* (Matthew 11:25)

This posture of humility does not exclude study; it sanctifies it. Scholarship without surrender becomes arrogance; devotion without discernment becomes superstition. The Spirit unites both head and heart so that knowledge leads to wisdom and truth produces transformation. Misunderstanding is healed not by cleverness but by communion. When the heart kneels, the mind sees.

Misunderstanding the nature of the Bible

A major cause of misunderstanding arises from forgetting what the Bible actually *is*. Many treat it as a moral handbook, a collection of inspirational sayings, or a historical record. While it contains moral instruction, wisdom, and history, its primary purpose is revelation.

It tells us who God is, what He has done, and how we are called to live in covenant relationship with Him. *"These are written that you may believe that Jesus is the Messiah, the Son of God, and that by believing you may have life in his name."* (John 20:31)

When readers approach Scripture for information rather than transformation, misunderstanding is inevitable. The Bible was never intended to be analysed apart from faith. Its truths are spiritually discerned, not merely intellectually decoded. *"The person without the Spirit does not accept the things that come from the Spirit of God... they are discerned only through the Spirit."* (1 Corinthians 2:14). This does not devalue study; it defines its purpose. The Bible is meant to lead to worship, not merely to knowledge.

The Spirit reminds believers that the Bible's unity and diversity both serve revelation. It is one book with many voices, one story told through many different forms. Those who read expecting contradiction often find it because they approach Scripture as critics rather than as recipients. The Bible will not yield its treasures to those who come to test it; it opens to those who come to trust it. The misunderstanding lies not in the text but in the posture of the reader.

Misunderstanding the Old and the New

A common misunderstanding in modern Christianity is the relationship between the Old and New Testaments. Some dismiss the Old as obsolete; others merge it so closely with the New that distinctions disappear. Both errors rob Scripture of its depth. Jesus said plainly, *"Do not think that I have come to abolish the Law or the Prophets; I have not come to abolish them but to fulfil them."* (Matthew 5:17). Fulfilment means continuity, it doesn't mean cancellation.

Misunderstanding arises when Christians apply Old Covenant commands without recognising their fulfilment in Christ. The sacrificial laws, for example, pointed forward to the perfect sacrifice of Jesus, the Lamb of God. To continue offering animal sacrifices would now be to deny the sufficiency of Christ. Likewise, misunderstanding occurs when believers ignore the moral principles of the Law under the guise of grace. The Spirit enables discernment, showing how the eternal moral nature of God still stands, even as the ceremonial forms have passed away.

Paul captures this harmony beautifully: *"Whatever was written in former days was written for our instruction, that through endurance and through the encouragement of the Scriptures we might have hope."* (Romans 15:4).

The Old Testament reveals the promise; the New Testament reveals the Person. The two together form one revelation, illuminated by the same Spirit. When readers understand this relationship, they discover that law and grace are not rivals but partners in revealing the righteousness of God.

Misunderstanding context and application

Another frequent misunderstanding arises when believers confuse the meaning of a passage with its application. Every verse has one intended meaning but countless applications. The Spirit enables discernment between the two.

For example, when God told Jeremiah, *"Before I formed you in the womb I knew you,"* (Jeremiah 1:5). He spoke specifically of the prophet's calling. The actual meaning belongs to Jeremiah's commission, but the principle - that God knows and calls His people - applies to all believers. To confuse the two is to lose precision; to separate them is to lose power.

Application divorced from meaning leads to misinterpretation; meaning without application leads to stagnation. The Spirit joins both. He anchors understanding in the original intention of the text and then breathes relevance into it for the present moment. That is why the Bible remains living and active - unchanging in truth yet ever-changing in its personal impact. The Spirit ensures that Scripture speaks to each generation without surrendering its original message.

Faithful readers learn to ask both questions: "What did this mean *then?*" and "What does this mean *now?*" The first guards against distortion; the second prevents detachment. The Spirit bridges both, ensuring that interpretation becomes incarnation. Misunderstanding fades when Scripture is allowed to speak for itself - through the same Spirit who first gave it.

Misunderstanding the role of experience

Modern readers often misunderstand the relationship between Scripture and personal experience. Many elevate subjective experience above biblical revelation, assuming that feelings or impressions carry equal authority. Others dismiss experience entirely, fearing emotional excess. Both extremes distort the truth. The Spirit affirms experience, but only when it flows from and aligns with the Word. *"Sanctify them by the truth; your word is truth."* (John 17:17)

When believers treat emotion as revelation, misunderstanding multiplies. God does indeed speak through impressions, circumstances, and inner conviction, but never in contradiction to His Word. The Spirit never competes with Scripture; He confirms it. Experience is the field where truth takes root, not the fountain from which truth flows. The Bible interprets our experiences, not the other way around.

However, rejecting experience altogether is equally misguided. The Word of God is meant to be lived and felt. David said, *"Taste and see that the Lord is good."* (Psalm 34:8). Truth unexperienced becomes theory; experience untested becomes deception. The Spirit unites both, ensuring that the heart and mind together bear witness to truth.

When experience bows to Scripture and Scripture blossoms through experience, understanding matures into intimacy. The Bible ceases to be an object of study and becomes the living voice of the God who still speaks.

Misunderstanding the work of the Spirit

Some misunderstand the Spirit's relationship to the Word by dividing what God has joined. They either exalt Scripture without dependence on the Spirit or exalt the Spirit apart from Scripture. Both lead to distortion. The Word without the Spirit becomes lifeless orthodoxy; the Spirit without the Word becomes unanchored enthusiasm. The two always work together. *"The Spirit gives life; the flesh counts for nothing. The words I have spoken to you – they are full of the Spirit and life."* (John 6:63)

Throughout church history, misunderstanding of the Spirit's role has birthed both cold formalism and reckless fanaticism. Formalism turns Scripture into a relic; fanaticism turns revelation into chaos.

The Spirit's true work is illumination - making the written Word living to the believer. He does not add new revelation that contradicts Scripture but opens hearts to grasp the revelation already given. *"When he, the Spirit of truth, comes, he will guide you into all the truth."* (John 16:13)

The Spirit's ministry is not to invent truth but to incarnate it. He bridges the gap between knowledge and obedience, between reading and revelation. Without Him, the Bible remains closed; with Him, it burns like fire in the bones. Misunderstanding ceases when believers see that every true encounter with the Spirit deepens their understanding of the Word, and every true encounter with the Word draws them nearer to the Spirit. The two are never rivals; they are partners in the believer's transformation.

Misunderstanding grace and law

Another common misunderstanding is the relationship between grace and law. Some claim that grace abolishes the law, while others cling to the law as a means of earning grace. Both miss the heart of the gospel. Grace fulfils what law commands. *"For the law was given through Moses; grace and truth came through Jesus Christ."* (John 1:17). The law reveals God's holiness; grace reveals His help. The law exposes sin; grace empowers obedience. The Spirit unites the two in perfect harmony.

When believers misunderstand this relationship, they either fall into legalism or licentiousness. Legalism misuses Scripture to control behaviour without changing our hearts. Licentiousness misuses grace to excuse sin rather than overcome it. Paul addressed both: *"Shall we go on sinning so that grace may increase? By no means!"* (Romans 6:1–2). Grace is not permission but power - the power to live what the law demanded but could never enable.

The Spirit transforms the believer's relationship to both law and grace. Under His guidance, obedience becomes delight rather than duty. *"I will put my Spirit in you and move you to follow my decrees."* (Ezekiel 36:27). The common misunderstanding that grace removes moral responsibility is healed when we see that grace *fulfils* it. The Spirit writes the law not on tablets of stone but on hearts of flesh. The result is holiness born not of fear but of freedom.

Misunderstanding the purpose of the church

One of the most serious misunderstandings of Scripture today concerns the purpose of the church. Some view the church primarily as a humanitarian organisation; others see it merely as a spiritual escape from the world. Both extremes arise when the Bible's vision for the church is misunderstood.

Jesus prayed, *"As you sent me into the world, I have sent them into the world."* (John 17:18). The church exists not to retreat from the world nor to conform to it, but to redeem it through witness and service. Misunderstanding occurs when believers substitute cultural activism for gospel proclamation or, conversely, personal piety for public engagement.

The Spirit-inspired purpose of the church is both - declaring truth and demonstrating love. *"You are the salt of the earth… You are the light of the world."* (Matthew 5:13–14). Salt preserves; light reveals. When the Word of God is rightly understood, the church becomes both prophetic and compassionate, proclaiming truth without arrogance and serving without compromise.

The Spirit keeps the church centred by keeping her rooted in Scripture. Misunderstanding fades when believers recognise that every act of service and every word of witness must flow from the gospel. The church does not invent her mission; she inherits it. She does not expand it by creativity but embodies it through faithfulness. The Spirit ensures that the mission born in the Word continues through the Word - until the whole earth knows the glory of God.

The misunderstanding of prosperity

One of the most prevalent modern distortions of Scripture is the so-called "prosperity gospel." It promises health, wealth, and success to those who demonstrate enough faith, give enough money, or speak enough positive words. This teaching misuses the Bible by isolating verses about blessing and then ignoring passages about suffering. It exchanges faith in Christ for faith in formulas. Paul's warning is clear: *"People of corrupt mind... think that godliness is a means to financial gain."* (1 Timothy 6:5)

The prosperity distortion misunderstands both the nature of blessing and the purpose of faith. In Scripture, blessing is relational before it is material - it flows from being reconciled to God, not rewarded by Him. Abraham's wealth was not proof of his faith; his faith was proven when he was willing to sacrifice Isaac. Job's integrity was not measured by his possessions but by his perseverance. Jesus promised the kingdom, not comfort: *"In this world you will have trouble. But take heart! I have overcome the world."* (John 16:33)

True prosperity is the presence of God, not the accumulation of goods. The Spirit exposes the lie that success is the sign of divine favour. Christ Himself suffered poverty, rejection, and crucifixion - and through those things brought salvation to the world. The cross, not the bank account, is the measure of God's blessing. Any interpretation of Scripture that bypasses suffering or glorifies greed misunderstands the very heart of the gospel.

The misunderstanding of suffering

Conversely, some believers misunderstand suffering as a sign of divine displeasure. They read hardship as punishment, forgetting that Scripture portrays suffering as both a reality of a fallen world and a tool in God's hand for spiritual growth. Peter wrote, *"Do not be surprised at the fiery ordeal that has come on you to test you, as though something strange were happening to you."* (1 Peter 4:12). The Spirit turns trials into training grounds for trust. Misunderstanding suffering leads to despair, resentment, or self-condemnation.

It blinds believers to the refining work of God in pain. Paul's testimony stands as the ultimate correction: *"We also glory in our sufferings, because we know that suffering produces perseverance; perseverance, character; and character, hope."* (Romans 5:3–4). Suffering is not the absence of God's favour but the arena of its deepest expression. The cross again becomes the pattern - God's greatest victory emerged from apparent defeat.

When believers interpret suffering through the lens of Scripture, they discover purpose amid pain. The Spirit gives understanding that pain is never wasted; it shapes us into Christ's likeness. The misunderstanding of suffering dissolves when faith sees that glory grows from grief. *"Though outwardly we are wasting away, yet inwardly we are being renewed day by day."* (2 Corinthians 4:16). The believer who reads suffering in context reads it with hope.

The misunderstanding of faith

Another widespread misunderstanding is the idea that faith itself has power apart from its object. Some teach that faith is a force that manipulates reality; others treat it as a fragile feeling easily lost. Both misrepresent the biblical truth. Faith's strength lies not in intensity but in direction.

Jesus said, *"If you have faith as small as a mustard seed, you can say to this mountain, 'Move from here to there,' and it will move."* (Matthew 17:20). The power lies not in the seed but in the soil - the God who hears.

Faith is not a spiritual currency used to purchase blessings but trust in the character of God regardless of outcome. The heroes of Hebrews 11 are commended not because everything went well for them, but because they trusted God when it did not. *"Some faced jeers and flogging, and even chains and imprisonment."* (Hebrews 11:36). True faith clings to God even when His purposes remain hidden.

When Scripture is misunderstood, faith becomes transactional rather than transformational. The Spirit corrects this by turning our gaze from results to relationship. Faith's purpose is not to control circumstances but to conform us to Christ.

When faith is rightly understood, believers cease striving for outcomes and start resting in obedience. Misunderstanding fades where trust deepens, and the believer learns to say, *"I know whom I have believed."* (2 Timothy 1:12)

The misunderstanding of freedom

Freedom is one of Scripture's most celebrated and most misunderstood themes. Many interpret Christian freedom as the right to do whatever one pleases, but the Bible defines freedom as the power to do what pleases God. Paul wrote, *"You, my brothers and sisters, were called to be free. But do not use your freedom to indulge the flesh; rather, serve one another humbly in love"* (Galatians 5:13) Freedom without obedience is just rebellion disguised as liberty.

When readers separate freedom from holiness, the result is moral chaos. The Spirit grants freedom not from authority but for righteousness. Misunderstanding freedom leads believers to call self-expression spirituality and independence maturity. Yet true liberty is found only in submission to the Lordship of Christ. *"Now the Lord is the Spirit, and where the Spirit of the Lord is, there is freedom."* (2 Corinthians 3:17)

Freedom rightly understood becomes worship - the joyful ability to serve God without fear and to love others without condition. It is not autonomy but alignment. The Spirit breaks the chains of sin, not the bonds of obedience. Misuse of freedom always results in bondage; true freedom always bears the fruit of holiness. *"But now that you have been set free from sin and have become slaves of God, the benefit you reap leads to holiness, and the result is eternal life."* (Romans 6:22)

The misunderstanding of unity

One of the most painful misunderstandings in the church arises when unity is confused with uniformity. Some assume that agreement on every issue is required for fellowship, while others mistake unity for mere tolerance that ignores truth. Both distort the biblical vision.

Jesus prayed, *"That all of them may be one, Father, just as you are in me and I am in you."* (John 17:21). The unity of the church mirrors the Trinity - diverse persons bound by love and truth.

Misunderstanding unity leads to division on one hand and compromise on the other. Legalism fractures the body by elevating non-essentials; relativism weakens it by abandoning essentials. The Spirit guards the church from both by anchoring unity in Christ Himself. *"There is one body and one Spirit... one Lord, one faith, one baptism."* (Ephesians 4:4–5). Unity is not achieved by erasing differences but by exalting the One who transcends them.

When believers read Scripture rightly, they discover that truth and love are not competitors but companions. *"Speaking the truth in love, we will grow to become in every respect the mature body of him who is the head, that is, Christ."*(Ephesians 4:15) The Spirit calls the church to unity of purpose rather than uniformity of opinion. Misunderstanding fades when believers realise that unity is not something we create; it is something we protect. *"Make every effort to keep the unity of the Spirit through the bond of peace."* (Ephesians 4:3)

The misunderstanding of mission

Closely related is the misunderstanding of mission. Some reduce mission to evangelism alone; others expand it until it loses all reference to salvation. Both misrepresent the Bible's vision. The gospel is both proclamation and transformation - announcing the good news of salvation and embodying it through justice, mercy, and love. Jesus declared, *"As the Father has sent me, I am sending you."* (John 20:21). The church's mission is therefore not optional but essential, not political but spiritual, yet profoundly public in its witness. The truth is, the church does not have a mission. Christ has a mission, and that mission has a church.

Misunderstanding mission turns the church inward or outward in excess. When inward, it becomes a closed community focused only on preservation; when outward without gospel grounding, it becomes a social movement without salvation.

The Holy Spirit restores balance by uniting message and ministry. *"Let your light shine before others, that they may see your good deeds and glorify your Father in heaven."* (Matthew 5:16). The Word sends the church out not to impress but to illuminate.

The Spirit ensures that mission flows from Scripture, not sentiment. The church's calling is not self-defined but Spirit-directed. Misunderstanding ends when believers realise that mission begins in worship - hearing God's Word before speaking it to the world. The Great Commission is not a project but a participation in God's ongoing redemption. *"Go and make disciples of all nations… teaching them to obey everything I have commanded you."* (Matthew 28:19–20)

The misunderstanding of revelation

Another deep misunderstanding arises when believers equate revelation with novelty. Some chase after new words from God while neglecting the Word already given. Yet Scripture declares itself sufficient. *"All Scripture is God-breathed and is useful for teaching, rebuking, correcting and training in righteousness."* (2 Timothy 3:16).

The Spirit still speaks today, but never in contradiction to what He has already spoken. Revelation continues in application, not addition.

The misunderstanding of revelation very often stems from impatience. People desire immediacy and excitement rather than faithful study. But the Spirit's voice is recognised in the same way it has always been - through Scripture illuminated, not replaced. Jesus promised, *"The Advocate, the Holy Spirit… will remind you of everything I have said to you."* (John 14:26). The Spirit is a reminder, not a revisionist.

Faithful reading guards against counterfeit revelations that flatter human ambition or justify personal desires. The Spirit calls the church to discernment rooted in the Word. Every genuine word from God echoes the written Word and exalts Jesus Christ. *"The testimony of Jesus is the spirit of prophecy."* (Revelation 19:10)

The Spirit's purpose in revelation is not to create spiritual celebrities but to cultivate spiritual maturity.

Returning to reverence

At the heart of all misuse and misunderstanding lies a loss of reverence. When the Bible becomes common, its message becomes confused. Familiarity without awe breeds distortion. The Word of God must be approached with trembling joy - the awareness that we stand on holy ground. Isaiah's response before God's voice remains the model: *"Then I heard the voice of the Lord saying, 'Whom shall I send?' And I said, 'Here am I. Send me!'"* (Isaiah 6:8)

Reverence restores perspective. It reminds us that Scripture is not a subject to be mastered but a mystery to be entered. The Spirit rekindles reverence by revealing the holiness behind every page - the God who still speaks, still saves, and still sanctifies. The misuse of Scripture ends not in argument but in adoration. When hearts bow, understanding rises.

The Spirit is leading the church in every generation back to this posture. Beyond debates and divisions, He whispers the same invitation: *"This is the one I esteem: he who is humble and contrite in spirit, and trembles at my word."* (Isaiah 66:2).

When reverence returns, truth flourishes. Misuse ceases where worship begins, and misunderstanding melts in the light of revelation. The Bible becomes once again what it has always been - the living, breathing Word of the living God, faithful, flawless, and forever true.

9. UNITY IN DIVERSITY

One story, many voices

One of the greatest wonders of the Bible is its astonishing unity. Across fifteen hundred years, over forty authors, multiple continents, and an extraordinary range of genres, the Scriptures speak with a single coherent voice about the character, purposes, and heart of God. No other collection of writings in human history shares this scope or harmony. The Bible is not a single book in the conventional sense; it is a Spirit-formed library, a tapestry woven across centuries in which each thread contributes to a unified revelation.

This unity is not artificial or imposed. It rises organically from the God who inspired the Scriptures. He is the One Author behind many authors, the one Truth speaking through many testimonies. This is why the Bible can begin with creation and end with new creation and remain a single divine story - a story that reveals God's heart through diverse human voices. The beauty of Scripture lies not in uniformity but in harmony, in the way the Spirit draws together different perspectives, genres, and personalities into a single melody of grace.

The Spirit behind the voices

The diversity of Scripture is undeniable. It contains narratives and laws, poetry and prophecy, wisdom sayings and letters, lament and celebration, apocalyptic visions and intimate pastoral counsel. Humanly speaking, these are radically different forms of communication.

Yet the Spirit breathes through them all. The same divine presence who inspired Moses also inspired David, Isaiah, Luke, Peter, and Paul. The same Spirit who moved through the ancient rhythms of Hebrew poetry spoke through the precision of Greek prose. This unity is not the result of editing or later manipulation; it is the fruit of the Spirit's sovereign guidance over centuries. As Peter wrote, *"For prophecy never had its origin in the human will, but prophets, though human, spoke from God as they were carried along by the Holy Spirit."* (2 Peter 1:21).

The phrase "carried along" reminds us that God did not override their personalities; He directed them. Each writer contributed authentically, yet the outcome bears a single divine signature. When we read Scripture, therefore, we encounter both the human and the divine - human voices speaking divine truth; human hearts expressing divine revelation. Diversity does not threaten inspiration; it displays it. Only the Spirit could orchestrate such harmony from such variety.

One message through many styles

Part of reading the Bible wisely is recognising the particular style and intention of each book. God communicated His truth in ways that best suited the message. Poetry carries emotion in ways narrative cannot. Law expresses holiness with clarity that poetry would obscure. Prophecy shakes the soul awake in a way pastoral letters do not. Jesus' parables conceal and reveal simultaneously, inviting deeper hunger. Paul's epistles cut through confusion with pastoral and theological precision.

This diversity is itself revelation. God chooses not to speak in one narrow form but through many voices, inviting readers from every culture and temperament to hear Him. A world that communicates through art, story, argument, and song needs a Bible that speaks in the same ways. The Spirit is endlessly wise in His choice of instruments.

Recognising this diversity protects us from reading everything the same way. Poetry cannot be forced into the mould of law. Apocalyptic imagery cannot be flattened into literal description. Narrative must not be treated as allegory unless the text itself suggests it. When we respect each form, we hear God more clearly.

A unified story of redemption

Despite its variety, the Bible tells one overarching story: the revelation of God's heart in the redemption of humanity. From Genesis to Revelation, Scripture moves toward Christ. The early chapters reveal a God who creates out of love, mourns over sin, and promises a Deliverer.

The prophets speak of a coming Messiah who will restore what was broken. The Gospels unveil that hope fulfilled in Jesus. The epistles explain the meaning of His work. Revelation reveals the completion of all things in Him.

This golden thread of Christ unifies the entire Scriptures. Jesus Himself said, *"These are the very Scriptures that testify about me."* (John 5:39). After His resurrection, He opened the disciples' minds to see that *"everything must be fulfilled that is written about me in the Law of Moses, the Prophets and the Psalms."* (Luke 24:44). The whole Bible is a single Christ-centred revelation. Its unity is not just literary or thematic; it is profoundly theological. The heart of God is revealed fully in Christ, and Scripture's diverse voices together proclaim Him.

Diversity that deepens, not dilutes

Some readers see the Bible's diversity and mistakenly conclude that it contradicts itself, or that its different voices represent competing theologies. But what appears at first glance as tension is usually the richness of multi-dimensional truth. Wisdom literature looks at life from the ground-up; prophetic literature looks from heaven-down. Paul writes with pastoral concern for scattered churches; James speaks with prophetic fire. Their voices differ, but their message resonates: God is holy, God is faithful, and God is redeeming His people.

The Spirit uses this diversity to deepen our understanding. If Scripture spoke only in one tone, our view of God would be shallow. Instead, He reveals His heart from many angles, using the full spectrum of human expression. Diversity does not dilute truth; it enriches it.

Where misreading begins

Many misunderstandings arise when readers ignore Scripture's diversity and force every text to say the same thing in the same way. Some treat poetry as literal law. Others turn prophecy into prediction charts. Others read letters without their context or flatten narratives into universal commands.

The misuse of Scripture often comes from misreading its forms. To hear God's heart, we must receive His revelation as He chose to give it - in varied forms, through different voices, shaped by the Spirit's wisdom. Unity in diversity is not a challenge to overcome but a gift to embrace.

One Spirit, many contexts

Every book of the Bible was written in a real place, at a real time, to real people. These contexts were as diverse as the cultures themselves: ancient Mesopotamia, the wilderness wanderings, Egypt, the monarchy of Israel, Babylonian exile, Second Temple Judaism, and the early Greco-Roman Church. Each setting shaped the form of the message, but not its truth. The Spirit inspired Scripture *within* human context, not apart from it. Just as Jesus entered a real culture when He became flesh, so God's Word entered real cultures when it became text.

Understanding this protects us from reading the Bible as if it fell out of the sky, untouched by history. Instead, we honour the Spirit by recognising the wisdom of the contexts He chose. God did not reveal Himself through abstraction but through lived human experience. When He wanted to speak of love, He inspired poetry. When He wanted to warn of judgment, He raised up prophets. When He wanted to show wisdom lived out, He inspired proverbs. When He wanted to teach the church, He guided apostles to write letters.

The unity of Scripture is not sameness but coherence — a single message expressed in many forms, each shaped by the culture in which the Spirit breathed. Appreciating context does not weaken Scripture's authority; it strengthens it. It helps us hear what God actually meant, rather than what we assume.

The harmony of the Testaments

One of the most remarkable demonstrations of unity in diversity is the harmony between the Old and New Testaments. Written centuries apart, in different languages and cultural worlds, they nevertheless form a single revelation.

The Old Testament lays the foundation; the New Testament builds upon it. The Old anticipates; the New fulfils. The Old reveals the problem; the New reveals the solution. The Old speaks of promise; the New reveals the Promised One.

Jesus affirmed this unity repeatedly. *"Do not think that I have come to abolish the Law or the Prophets; I have not come to abolish them but to fulfil them."* (Matthew 5:17). The early church saw Christ not as a departure from Scripture but as its centre. The law, the prophets, the psalms, the stories - all pointed to Him.

When readers treat the Testaments as competing or contradictory, they miss the Spirit's symphony. The diversity of the two Testaments displays the progressive nature of revelation: God revealing His heart in stages, through history, until the fullness of time in Christ. Unity in diversity is the very structure of the Bible itself.

Complementary perspectives, not conflicting voices

The Bible's diverse genres and perspectives often lead modern readers to ask whether the Scriptures disagree with themselves. This question arises not because the text is inconsistent, but because we sometimes expect it to speak in one voice rather than many.

For example, the books of Kings and Chronicles describe many of the same events, yet with different emphases. Kings focuses on political decline; Chronicles focuses on spiritual hope. Their perspectives differ, but together they give a fuller picture. The four Gospels recount the life of Jesus with unique details and emphases. John tells us that Jesus did far more than could be written. *"But these are written that you may believe that Jesus is the Messiah, the Son of God."* (John 20:31). Each Gospel writer, guided by the Spirit, selected what would best serve their audience and purpose.

The diversity of these various accounts does not undermine trustworthiness - it strengthens it. Multiple angles confirm the truth, just as multiple witnesses confirm an event.

Variety enriches credibility. God entrusted the story of His Son not to a single storyteller but to four Spirit-inspired witnesses, each contributing to a unified portrait of Christ.

The unity of doctrine

Doctrine, too, reflects unity in diversity. The teaching of Scripture is not delivered as a systematic textbook but as a living tapestry. Paul's profound theological arguments stand alongside the practical wisdom of James. John speaks of love with poetic fire, while Peter speaks of endurance with the weight of pastoral suffering. Yet their message is one: God is holy, God is love, God is faithful, and salvation is found in Christ alone.

When believers isolate one voice and ignore the others, distortions arise. Some cling to Paul while neglecting James or cherish the gospels while overlooking the prophets. But the Spirit gave all these voices for our good.

Sound doctrine emerges not from select passages but from the whole counsel of God. The unity of truth is found in the harmony of many inspired perspectives.

Unity and the interpreter's responsibility

Because Scripture is diverse, the interpreter has a sacred responsibility: to read each part in light of the whole and the whole in light of Christ. No verse stands alone. No book has its own independent theology. The diversity of Scripture demands careful listening — listening with humility, attentiveness, and submission to the Spirit.

Misinterpretation often arises when readers separate texts from their broader scriptural context. A single proverb cannot override the message of the prophets. A symbolic vision in Revelation cannot overturn the clear teaching of Jesus. The Spirit who inspired the whole Bible helps us read the whole Bible. When we allow Scripture to interpret Scripture, unity emerges from diversity. This is why engaging with the Bible requires patience.

It invites us into a lifelong conversation with the Spirit, who reveals truth progressively, layer by layer. Quick readings produce shallow conclusions. Deep readings, guided by the Spirit, reveal God's heart.

Why unity in diversity matters today

The modern world is fragmented. Opinions compete, voices clash, and truth feels elusive. In such a world, the Bible stands as a testimony to God's unchanging heart expressed through many different human voices. Its unity reveals divine authorship; its diversity reveals divine generosity.

God speaks to scholars and shepherds, kings and exiles, poets and fishermen. He speaks through lament and celebration, through vision and instruction. The Bible's diversity invites every reader into the story.

More importantly, unity in diversity protects the Church from error. When we pick and choose from Scripture to support our preferences, we create an echo chamber shaped in our own image. But when we submit to the full range of Scripture's voices, we are shaped by God's heart rather than our own. The diversity of Scripture humbles us; its unity anchors us.

The Spirit who unifies the reader

Just as the Spirit unified the writers, He unifies the readers. Across cultures, denominations, and languages, believers recognise the same divine voice speaking through Scripture. This unity is not uniformity; it is shared submission to the Spirit's revelation. The same Spirit who breathed truth into the hearts of the prophets now breathes understanding into the hearts of those who read in faith.

Paul prayed that the church would experience this unity of understanding through the Spirit: *"May the God who gives endurance and encouragement give you the same attitude of mind toward each other that Christ Jesus had."* (Romans 15:5). The unity of Scripture leads to unity in the church - not by erasing the differences but by grounding us in shared truth.

The whole Bible for the whole life

Ultimately, unity in diversity reveals a God who engages the whole person - mind, heart, imagination, community, justice, worship and hope. No single genre or perspective can carry the fullness of His revelation. He speaks to every part of life because He seeks every part of us.

This chapter, placed here, serves a crucial purpose: it gathers the threads of Scripture into one coherent portrait of God's heart. Before we explore how to hear God today, we must grasp the wisdom of how He has spoken - through many voices, yet with one Spirit; through many forms, yet with one message; through many centuries, yet with one heart.

Unity in diversity is not simply a description of the Bible. It is the posture we must bring to the Bible - receiving each text in its uniqueness, trusting the Spirit who brings them together, and listening for the divine heartbeat that echoes through them all.

10. HEARING GOD IN THE BIBLE

The God who still speaks through His Word

The God of Scripture is not silent. He has always been a God who speaks - creating by His voice, calling His people by His voice, correcting and comforting by His voice. The Bible is the record of that divine speech, preserved by the Spirit, and still alive with His presence. When we speak of hearing God today, we are not reaching for something mysterious or rare. We are referring to the most ordinary miracle in the Christian life: the Spirit opening our hearts to hear the voice of God in the words He inspired.

In an age when many pursue spiritual experiences, prophetic impressions, or inner promptings, it is vital to say clearly that the primary, normative, and trustworthy way God speaks today is through Scripture. This does not diminish the Spirit's personal activity; rather, it honours the very instrument the Spirit chose to reveal God's heart. To hear God today is to encounter the living voice of the Spirit in the text He breathed out.

The writer of Hebrews declares, *"The word of God is alive and active. Sharper than any double-edged sword…"*(Hebrews 4:12). To be "alive" is to be present. To be "active" is to be speaking. When Christians read Scripture with humility and faith, they discover a profound truth: God is not merely *recorded* there, He is *present* there.

The Spirit Who illuminates the Scriptures

The same Spirit who inspired the Scriptures now illuminates them. Illumination is not new revelation; it is the Spirit opening our hearts to understand what He has already spoken. Paul writes, *"We have received… the Spirit who is from God, so that we may understand what God has freely given us."* (1 Corinthians 2:12).

Understanding is a gift. Clarity is an act of grace. Insight is a work of the Spirit. When believers open the Bible, the Spirit translates divine truth into living understanding. He takes ancient words and applies them to present life.

He convicts, guides, comforts, and challenges - not by adding to Scripture but by awakening us to its meaning. The disciples on the road to Emmaus described how their hearts burned as Jesus explained the Scriptures to them. That burning continues wherever the Spirit enlightens the people of God.

Hearing God begins with humility

The posture of the heart determines whether we hear God at all. Pride deafens. Hurry distracts. Preconceptions distort. Scripture is not a book to conquer but a revelation to receive. The Spirit speaks most clearly when we come with humility – which means our acknowledging His authority, confessing our blindness, and asking Him to open the Scriptures to our understanding. The psalmist prayed, *"Open my eyes that I may see wonderful things in your law."* (Psalm 119:18). The Holy Spirit honours that prayer in every generation.

Humility also means recognising our limitations. We read Scripture within our culture, language, experiences, and assumptions. Without the Spirit's help, we inevitably read into the text what we want to find. Many misunderstandings of Scripture come not from malice but from unexamined assumptions. Hearing God today means surrendering these assumptions and letting the Spirit reshape our thoughts around God's truth rather than shaping God's truth around our thoughts.

Hearing God requires patience and attention

We live in a hurried age, where speed is celebrated and silence is rare. But the voice of God in Scripture is often heard slowly, like seeds taking root. Spiritual clarity does not come to distracted minds. The Spirit speaks through reflection, meditation, and the deep listening of a patient heart.

The psalmist describes the blessed person as one who meditates on God's law *"day and night"* - lingering long enough for truth to seep into the soul. When we rush through Scripture, we often walk past the very words where God desires to meet us.

Hearing God today means making space - space for Scripture to breathe, space for silence to settle, space for the Spirit to bring meaning to mind. A hurried reader hears little. A listening reader hears much.

Hearing God through right interpretation

The Spirit does not override the need for careful interpretation; He empowers it. He guides us into truth, but He does so through the very methods that honour the text - understanding context, genre, historical setting, and authorial intent. The Spirit does not bless careless reading. He blesses faithful reading.

Jesus rebuked the religious leaders for failing to understand Scripture properly. *"You are in error because you do not know the Scriptures or the power of God."* (Matthew 22:29). Error arises both from ignorance of the text and ignorance of the Spirit's power. Truth requires both.

When we read Scripture as it was meant to be read - respecting its context, receiving its diversity, recognising its unity - we hear God more clearly. The Spirit never leads us away from the meaning already present in Scripture; He leads us deeper into it.

Hearing God within community

God never intended Scripture to be heard in isolation alone. From Israel's public readings to the early church's gatherings, the Spirit has always spoken powerfully through the community of believers. Paul reminded Timothy that Scripture is profitable for *"teaching and training in righteousness"* - communal activities shaped by shared submission to God's Word.

Hearing God today includes listening to the wisdom of the church - past and present. The Spirit who leads us is the same Spirit who has led believers across centuries.

Tradition does not replace Scripture, but it safeguards us from the arrogance of believing we are the first to understand it. The Spirit unites believers in a shared recognition of truth.

When people say "God Told Me…"

This is one of the most important pastoral issues of our time. Many sincere Christians use the phrase *"God told me…"* to describe a strong feeling, an impression, a thought, or a sense of direction. While God certainly guides His people, we must be careful not to elevate subjective impressions to the level of Scripture.

The Spirit will never contradict Himself. He inspired the Bible; therefore, He will never speak in ways that undermine or bypass it. Any impression that violates Scripture cannot come from the Spirit. John warns, *"Dear friends, do not believe every spirit, but test the spirits to see whether they are from God."* (1 John 4:1). The test is the Word.

Personal impressions are real, but they must remain personal - not authoritative for others, and never equal to Scripture. They must be tested by Scripture, submitted to wisdom, and held with humility. When believers treat impressions as revelation, confusion and spiritual harm follow quickly. When they treat impressions as prompts to be weighed by Scripture, the Spirit guides safely.

The Spirit's leading in the believer's life is gentle, subtle, and always anchored in Scripture. He may nudge us toward forgiveness, generosity, courage, or prayer - but such nudges never express new doctrine, foretell new truth, or add to God's revelation.

False certainty and the danger of subjective "words"

One of the greatest dangers in contemporary Christianity is the shift from *"God has spoken in Scripture"* to *"God is speaking new things to me."* Scripture thereby becomes optional, and personal impressions become ultimate. This reverses the order the Spirit Himself established. A church that elevates impressions above Scripture becomes vulnerable to manipulation, delusion, and division. Many have been spiritually wounded by someone claiming, *"God told me…"* when God said nothing of the sort.

The Spirit never bypasses the Bible to whisper secrets into a single person's ear. He speaks through the Word He Himself inspired. To hear God today, therefore, is to discern the difference between divine truth and human imagination. The Spirit gives wisdom to tell the difference. He leads us back to Scripture, never away from it. What He once breathed out, He continues to illuminate — and that is the safe, sure ground upon which Christians can stand.

The transforming voice of Scripture

Hearing God in Scripture is never meant to be a passive experience. Divine speech shapes those who receive it. The prophets trembled. The psalmist rejoiced. The disciples' hearts burned. Every genuine encounter with God's voice produces transformation - conviction that leads to repentance, comfort that leads to trust, and instruction that leads to obedience. James warns believers not to deceive themselves by hearing the Word without doing it. *"Do not merely listen to the word and so deceive yourselves. Do what it says."* (James 1:22). Obedience is the evidence of hearing.

This is why reading Scripture devotionally is not simply about inspiration but formation. The Word does not flatter us; it reshapes us. It reveals our hidden motives, exposes our idols, awakens our hope, confronts our pride, and draws us deeper into the character of Christ. The Spirit speaks through the Word not merely to inform the mind but to reform the heart.

The world around us speaks constantly, shaping our fears and desires. But when God speaks through Scripture, His voice calls us into a new reality — the reality of His kingdom. To hear God today is to enter into the life He offers and yield to the work He is doing. Scripture is more than a message; it is a means of grace by which the Spirit transforms us into the likeness of Christ.

The Bible as the Spirit's primary instrument

The Bible is not simply one of many ways God speaks; it is the foundation upon which all other forms of guidance rest.

Dreams, impressions, counsel, and circumstances may point us toward God's purposes, but they must always be tested against the clarity of Scripture. The Spirit never leads contrary to the Word He inspired. This foundational principle safeguards the church from error and believers from confusion.

When believers feel led in a particular direction, Scripture becomes the anchor that ensures discernment. It settles the heart when emotions run high. It clarifies God's character when uncertainty clouds the mind. It restrains presumptions and corrects misunderstandings. When the Spirit guides, He guides through the truth He has revealed in Scripture, not apart from it. Jesus promised that the Spirit would *"guide you into all the truth."* (John 16:13). This guiding is not the unveiling of new revelations but the deepening of understanding of the truth already given.

The Spirit takes what Christ has made known and applies it freshly and powerfully to the believer's life. This is how God continues to speak today - not by bypassing His Word, but by illuminating it.

The danger of hearing without discerning

Not every voice that stirs the heart is from God. The human mind generates powerful internal impressions; human emotions can feel like spiritual impulses; and human desire can masquerade as divine leading. These experiences are real, but their source must be discerned. John warns, *"Do not believe every spirit, but test the spirits."* (1 John 4:1). The test is always the Word of God.

Discerning the difference between God's prompting and our own desires requires wisdom, maturity, and submission to Scripture. The Spirit does not stir disordered desires, sow confusion, or contradict God's revealed character. If an impression leads to pride, fear, resentment, entitlement, or self-promotion, it must be rejected. If it leads to humility, holiness, service, and submission to Christ, it may well be the Spirit's prompting - but even then, Scripture remains the final judge.

This vigilance is not meant to create suspicion but to cultivate spiritual maturity. The Spirit does not shame those who misinterpret impressions; He teaches them. He leads believers not into perfect accuracy but into a much deeper dependence. Discernment is a journey, not a moment. It is learned over time as Scripture forms the mind of Christ within us.

Hearing God together

As already mentioned above, the Holy Spirit speaks powerfully through the gathered community of believers. I really want to emphasise this. When the Bible is read, preached, discussed, and prayed together, the Spirit often works in ways He does not in private. This is by design. Christianity is a communal faith. The Spirit indwells the individual, but He also indwells the body. Paul reminds us in 1 Corinthians 2:16, that *"we have the mind of Christ."* Not "I" alone, but "we" together.

When the church submits to Scripture within the unity of the community, false interpretations are corrected, and blind spots are revealed. No individual possesses perfect understanding. But together, under the Spirit's guidance, the church discerns the truth with remarkable clarity. This is why believers need the preaching of the Word, the wisdom of elders, and the insights of the global and historical church. The Spirit who inspired Scripture does not isolate believers; He unites them through their shared submission to the Word.

The Spirit's whisper within the word

Modern Christians often long for the dramatic: the audible voice, the miraculous sign, the unmistakable moment of clarity. God can do such things, but they are rare in Scripture and never the foundation of faith. The great movements of God's people did not depend on spectacular revelations but on steadfast obedience to the Word already given. Elijah discovered this on the mountain. God was not in the wind, the earthquake, or the fire. He was in the gentle whisper. The whisper was not vague intuition; it was the intimate voice of God calling His servant back to purpose.

Today, that whisper is heard most clearly in the Bible. When Scripture is opened with faith, the Spirit whispers truth directly to the heart - sometimes comforting, sometimes confronting, always revealing God's character.

The whisper is a testimony of relationship. The Spirit speaks softly because He is close. He speaks through Scripture because Scripture is the living record of God's heart. Hearing God today means learning to recognise that quiet voice within the consistent, trustworthy, and Spirit-filled words of Scripture.

The silence that speaks

There are seasons when God feels silent, even when we faithfully read Scripture. These seasons are not abandonment but invitation. Silence invites deeper trust. Silence purifies motives. Silence tests our dependence. Silence draws us closer to God not by removing His Word but by deepening our hunger for it.

In these moments, the Spirit is still at work. He may highlight a single phrase, stir an unexpected memory of Scripture, or remind us of a truth we have overlooked. Often, however, His work is internal, unnoticed until later - shaping our desires, steadying our hearts, strengthening our faith. When God seems silent, He often speaks most profoundly through the very Word we are struggling to understand.

The Word that becomes life

God's Word is not simply heard; it is lived. The Spirit forms Christ in us by shaping our lives according to the Word. Jesus described this transformation as house-building. Hearing without obedience is building on sand. Hearing with obedience is building on rock. *"Everyone who hears these words of mine and puts them into practice..."* (Matthew 7:24). The Spirit ensures that hearing becomes doing, and doing becomes Christlikeness.

Hearing God today means allowing Scripture to confront our sin, shape our ethics, influence our relationships, govern our decisions, and direct our steps.

It means letting the Spirit apply the Word to our daily lives, not merely our minds. The Bible was never meant to remain on the page. It was meant to become flesh in the lives of those who believe.

The Spirit's witness in the believer

One of the Spirit's most profound ministries is His internal witness that confirms the truth of Scripture. Paul describes this as the Spirit bearing witness with our spirit - affirming that we are children of God. This internal affirmation is not new revelation but deep assurance. When believers read Scripture, the Spirit whispers, *"This is true."* When they face temptation, He whispers, *"This is not your path."* When they are uncertain, He whispers, *"Trust Me."*

This witness is always tied to Scripture. It is not vague spirituality but the Spirit interpreting and applying God's Word to the believer's soul. It is a personal, experiential confirmation of biblical truth - the living reality of God speaking through His Word.

From hearing to doing

To hear God today is to listen to Scripture with faith, humility, and attentiveness - but hearing is only the beginning. The Spirit does not illuminate the Word merely to inform our minds but to transform our lives. Every word God speaks calls for a response. Jesus declared, *"Everyone who hears these words of mine and puts them into practice is like a wise man who built his house on the rock."* (Matthew 7:24). Hearing becomes wisdom only when it becomes obedience.

This is why the Spirit speaks through Scripture: not to entertain our curiosity or satisfy our intellect, but to shape our character, reorder our desires, confront our sins, and lead us into the life God intends. The voice of God is not background noise to our discipleship; it is the very substance of it. When the Spirit opens our hearts to understand the Word, He is also inviting us to live that Word with courage and faithfulness.

Hearing God today, then, prepares us for the next and necessary step: living out what He reveals. The Scriptures we read with open hearts must become the Scriptures we embody with open lives. Illumination leads to transformation, and transformation produces obedience. The Spirit who speaks through the Word is the same Spirit who empowers us to live it.

And so, having considered how we hear God through Scripture, we turn to the essential question that follows: What does it mean to live the Word? This is the heartbeat of discipleship - where revelation becomes formation, and where the voice of God becomes the shape of a life.

11. LIVING THE WORD

Hearing God through Scripture is a sacred gift, but it is only the beginning. The Word of God is not given for admiration alone; it is given for embodiment. Revelation always calls for response, and understanding always invites obedience.

If the last chapter showed us how the Spirit helps us hear the voice of God in the Scriptures, this chapter shows us how the Spirit empowers us to live that voice in daily life. For the Bible is not merely a text to be studied - it is a truth to be lived, a calling to be embraced, and a life to be formed in us by the Spirit who breathed it.

From the opening pages of Scripture, God's revelation has never been intended merely for admiration but for action. Truth demands transformation. When God speaks, He expects His people to respond.

"Do not merely listen to the word and so deceive yourselves. Do what it says." (James 1:22). To hear the Word without living it is spiritual self-deception - like gazing into a mirror and walking away unchanged.

The great danger in every generation of the church is that biblical knowledge can outpace obedience. We become experts in theology but novices in love. Yet Jesus made it clear in John 14:15 that the true test of discipleship is not how much we know but how faithfully we live what we know. *"If you love me, keep my commands."* Obedience is the language of love; it translates belief into behaviour.

Living the Word is not about earning God's favour - it is the evidence of having received it. Grace does not make obedience optional; it makes it possible. The same Spirit who inspired Scripture empowers believers to live it. What God commands, He enables. The Word gives direction; the Spirit gives power. Together they form the divine partnership that turns truth into transformation.

2. The Word in the heart

Before the Word can shape our actions, it must first saturate our hearts. The psalmist prayed, *"I have hidden your word in my heart that I might not sin against you."* (Psalm 119:11). Scripture stored within becomes strength in temptation, comfort in sorrow, and wisdom in confusion. To live the Word externally, we must first internalise it. Memorisation and meditation are not religious exercises but spiritual nutrition - feeding the soul until truth becomes instinct.

When the heart is filled with the Word, the Spirit has material to work with. He brings to remembrance promises, warnings, and encouragements precisely when they are needed. A mind renewed by Scripture becomes a reservoir of divine perspective.

This is why Paul urged believers, *"Let the message of Christ dwell among you richly."* (Colossians 3:16). Dwelling richly means the Word takes residence, not visitation - it becomes the permanent environment of our thoughts.

Living the Word, therefore, begins in private devotion. Before we can speak truth publicly, we must soak in it privately. A day started in the Word often ends in obedience; a day begun in distraction rarely does. The Spirit delights to meet the believer whose heart is open and whose Bible is open. Living the Word flows not from human effort but from daily exposure to divine influence.

The Word in the mind

Transformation begins when the mind is renewed. *"Do not conform to the pattern of this world but be transformed by the renewing of your mind."* (Romans 12:2). The Spirit uses Scripture to reshape our thinking - challenging lies, correcting assumptions, and aligning priorities. Living the Word means learning to think as God thinks. Before behaviour changes, belief must change; before we act differently, we must see differently. The battle for obedience is often won or lost in the mind. When temptation whispers, it appeals to thoughts not yet surrendered.

The Spirit counters with truth hidden in memory. Jesus Himself modelled this during His temptation in the wilderness. Each time the enemy twisted Scripture, Jesus replied with what was written: *"It is written: 'Man shall not live on bread alone, but on every word that comes from the mouth of God.'"* (Matthew 4:4). The Living Word overcame the lie with the written Word.

As we meditate on Scripture, the Spirit trains our minds to discern truth from error. Biblical thinking becomes spiritual reflex. Over time, our thoughts begin to echo God's thoughts, and our desires reflect His desires. Living the Word is not about suppressing sin through discipline alone but replacing deception with revelation. When the mind is renewed, holiness becomes natural rather than forced.

The Word in the mouth

To live the Word also means to speak it. Faith is vocal; truth is contagious. *"The mouth speaks what the heart is full of."* (Luke 6:45). If the heart overflows with Scripture, the mouth will overflow with grace and truth. Every conversation will then become an opportunity to sow seeds of life. Living the Word in speech means our words carry the fragrance of heaven even in ordinary dialogue.

The early church understood the power of a Word-filled witness. *"Those who had been scattered preached the word wherever they went."* (Acts 8:4). They were not professional preachers but ordinary believers whose hearts burned with the message of Christ. When the Word saturates a person, it inevitably spills over. Evangelism is less about technique and more about overflow. Living the Word means letting Scripture shape both what we say and how we say it.

This includes the ministry of encouragement. Words guided by Scripture can heal, restore, and strengthen others. A single verse shared in love can lift a soul from despair. *"Let your conversation be always full of grace, seasoned with salt, so that you may know how to answer everyone."* (Colossians 4:6)

Speaking the Word is not about quoting verses mechanically but about expressing the heart of God with genuine humility and compassion. The Spirit turns ordinary speech into instruments of grace.

The Word in the hands

Obedience must ultimately move from heart and mind to hands and feet. The gospel that fills our thoughts must also shape our actions. James declared, *"Faith by itself, if it is not accompanied by action, is dead."* (James 2:17). True faith always acts. Living the Word means allowing Scripture to direct all our conduct in business, relationships, service, and sacrifice. Every decision becomes a canvas for divine obedience.

Jesus portrayed this vividly in the parable of the wise and foolish builders. *"Everyone who hears these words of mine and puts them into practice is like a wise man who built his house on the rock."* (Matthew 7:24). The storm came to both houses, but only the doer's house stood firm. The strength of our foundation is revealed not in calm weather but in crisis. Living the Word builds resilience that withstands life's tempests.

The Spirit empowers practical holiness. When the Word commands generosity, the Spirit enables giving; when it calls for forgiveness, the Spirit provides grace; when it demands courage, the Spirit imparts strength. Living the Word is the Spirit's masterpiece - a life that looks like Jesus because it listens like Jesus. As John reminds us, *"Whoever claims to live in him must live as Jesus did."* (1 John 2:6)

The Word in the church

Living the Word is never a solitary pursuit. The Bible was given to the community of faith, and it flourishes in the context of fellowship. The Spirit works through the Body to bring the Word to life among believers. *"Let the message of Christ dwell among you richly as you teach and admonish one another with all wisdom."* (Colossians 3:16). The church then becomes a living commentary on Scripture - each member interpreting truth through love and obedience.

When the Word governs the church, unity thrives. Disputes are settled not by personality but by principle. Worship is grounded in truth, and mission flows naturally from it. The Spirit uses the shared Word to weave hearts together in common purpose. *"Make every effort to keep the unity of the Spirit through the bond of peace."* (Ephesians 4:3). Living the Word corporately means letting Scripture shape how we relate, serve, and forgive within the Body of Christ.

The church also becomes a witness to the world when she lives the Word. A congregation that embodies Scripture speaks louder than any sermon. The early believers were described as *"devoted to the apostles' teaching and to fellowship."* (Acts 2:42). Teaching produced transformation; doctrine became discipleship. The Holy Spirit still calls today's church to be not just a preaching community but a practicing one - where truth is seen as well as heard.

The Word in the world

Living the Word extends beyond the sanctuary into the streets. Jesus prayed, *"As you sent me into the world, I have sent them into the world."* (John 17:18). The same Word that sanctifies the believer sends them on mission. Scripture is not a retreat from reality but a resource for engagement. The Spirit empowers believers to embody the gospel in workplaces, neighbourhoods, and nations.

The world does not need more Bible critics; it needs more Bible carriers - men and women whose lives display the truth they profess. Living the Word means translating doctrine into deeds of mercy and justice. Remember the words of Jesus, *"Let your light shine before others, that they may see your good deeds and glorify your Father in heaven."* (Matthew 5:16). The Word lived out becomes the most persuasive form of proclamation.

The Spirit sends us as living epistles - letters from God written to a watching world. *"You show that you are a letter from Christ… written not with ink but with the Spirit of the living God."* (2 Corinthians 3:3)

Every act of kindness, forgiveness, or integrity becomes a verse in that living letter. When believers live the Word in the world, Scripture walks on two legs, and Christ becomes visible through His people.

The Word and the will of God

Many Christians seek God's will as if it were hidden behind a veil, yet Scripture reveals it plainly. *"Your word is a lamp for my feet, a light on my path."* (Psalm 119:105). The Spirit uses the Word to guide choices, clarify callings, and align desires with divine purpose. Living the Word means making decisions consistent with God's revealed principles rather than chasing mystical signs.

Obedience to known truth should always precede any revelation of unknown truth. God's guidance unfolds step by step, not all at once. *"In all your ways submit to him, and he will make your paths straight."* (Proverbs 3:6). The Spirit does not bypass Scripture when leading believers; He applies it. Every verse obeyed opens the door to further direction. The safest way to discern God's will is to live the Word already given.

When believers anchor their choices in Scripture, confusion gives way to confidence. The Spirit transforms duty into delight, so obedience becomes the natural rhythm of life rather than a burdensome rule. Living the Word aligns will and worship - choosing God's ways because we love His heart.

The Word and the hope of glory

Living the Word not only shapes present behaviour but prepares believers for eternal destiny. The Scriptures point us beyond this life to the life to come. *"The world and its desires pass away, but whoever does the will of God lives forever."*(1 John 2:17). Each act of obedience sows seeds for eternity. The Spirit uses the Word to cultivate holiness that will one day be perfected in glory. When Christ returns, He will not measure success by knowledge amassed but by faith expressed through love. *"Well done, good and faithful servant."* (Matthew 25:23)

Those words will be spoken to those who not only heard but lived the Word. Scripture prepares believers for that moment, training hearts to long for His appearing and lives to reflect His character. Living the Word now is rehearsal for eternity.

Until that day, the Spirit continues His patient work of forming Christ within us through the Word. Every page we obey becomes a step toward the likeness of Jesus. The same Word that once called light out of darkness will call us from mortality into immortality. Living the Word is not just duty - it is destiny.

Living letters of grace

At last, the purpose of the Bible and the work of the Spirit converge in this one reality: God's people become the living expression of His Word. The written revelation produces living revelation - Christ seen in His church. As Paul said, *"You yourselves are our letter, written on our hearts, known and read by everyone."* (2 Corinthians 3:2). The world reads the gospel not only in Bibles but in believers. This is the outcome of all Scripture study, all theology, all preaching and prayer - that the Word becomes flesh again through us. The Spirit who inspired the prophets now indwells the saints, continuing God's message in human form. Living the Word means allowing the Author to keep writing His story through our lives. It is grace in motion, truth embodied, and love displayed.

The call of this final chapter is simple yet profound: let the Word you have read become the life you live. Let Scripture move from the page to the person, from text to testimony. When the Bible is both believed and embodied, it ceases to be merely a book - it becomes a bridge between heaven and earth.

The Word and the spirit of compassion

To live the Word is to live the love it reveals. The heart of Scripture is not argument but affection - God's compassion expressed through His Son. *"Be kind and compassionate to one another, forgiving each other, just as in Christ God forgave you."* (Ephesians 4:32)

The Spirit forms this compassion in believers so that the Word becomes visible not in debates but in deeds of mercy. Knowledge without love hardens; obedience rooted in love heals. When the Spirit fills the believer, biblical conviction is always clothed in grace.

Jesus embodied perfect truth and perfect compassion, never compromising either. He wept at Lazarus's tomb even though He knew resurrection was moments away. To live the Word means entering the pain of others while holding the promise of God.

The Spirit empowers compassion that costs. True love interrupts schedules, crosses boundaries, and serves enemies. *"Let us not love with words or speech but with actions and in truth."* (1 John 3:18). Living the Word means allowing God's compassion to move our hands and reorder our priorities until love becomes our reflex.

The Word and integrity of life

Living the Word requires integrity, an inner consistency between what we profess and what we practise. Scripture calls this "walking in the truth." *"I have no greater joy than to hear that my children are walking in the truth."* (3 John 1:4). Integrity means that our private world aligns with our public witness. The same Word that instructs the mind also inspects the motives.

The Holy Spirit will use Scripture as a mirror, revealing hidden inconsistencies and inviting repentance. David prayed, *"Search me, God, and know my heart; test me and know my anxious thoughts."* (Psalm 139:23). Living the Word demands that we welcome such searching. It is not self-condemnation but spiritual calibration - allowing the Spirit to bring every part of life under the authority of truth.

Integrity gives the gospel credibility. The world recognises authenticity more readily than rhetoric. When believers live transparently, confess sin quickly, and forgive freely, Scripture gains a hearing. The Spirit writes integrity into our lives one honest choice at a time until holiness becomes habit.

The Word and the discipline of service

The Bible never separates spirituality from servanthood. Jesus declared in Matthew 23:11, *"The greatest among you will be your servant."* To live the Word is to embrace humility as the posture of power. The Spirit transforms ambition into availability, turning knowledge of Scripture into acts of kindness.

Every command to love one another, bear one another's burdens, and wash one another's feet is the Word made practical. The Spirit equips each believer with gifts that translate doctrine into deeds. *"Each of you should use whatever gift you have received to serve others, as faithful stewards of God's grace in its various forms."* (1 Peter 4:10). Living the Word means discovering that ministry is not a role for a few but a responsibility for all.

Service is where theology meets humanity. It is easy to admire Christ's humility in theory but far harder to imitate it in practice. Yet the Spirit's presence turns obligation into joy. When we serve in His strength, fatigue becomes fulfilment because the Word we obey is alive within us.

The Word and the stewardship of resources

Scripture speaks as clearly about generosity as it does about faith. *"You will be enriched in every way so that you can be generous on every occasion."* (2 Corinthians 9:11). Living the Word means recognising that everything we possess is entrusted, not owned. The Spirit loosens our grip on material things so that the Word can reshape our relationship with wealth.

Generosity is not measured by amount but by attitude. The widow's two coins outweighed the riches of the Pharisees because they were given in faith. *"Where your treasure is, there your heart will be also."* (Matthew 6:21)

When the Word governs the wallet, greed loses its grip and gratitude grows. Stewardship also extends beyond money to time, talents, and influence.

The Spirit teaches believers to invest each resource in ways that echo eternity. Every act of generosity becomes a sermon without words. Living the Word in stewardship proclaims that God Himself is the giver of all good things, and our giving mirrors His heart.

The Word and the pursuit of justice

To live the Word is to stand where Scripture stands - on the side of righteousness, mercy, and truth. *"Learn to do right; seek justice. Defend the oppressed."* (Isaiah 1:17). Justice is not a political slogan but a spiritual calling. The Spirit compels believers to confront systems of sin as courageously as they confront personal sin.

Jesus announced His mission in the words of Isaiah: *"The Spirit of the Lord is on me, because he has anointed me to proclaim good news to the poor... to set the oppressed free."* (Luke 4:18). That same Spirit sends the church to continue His ministry. Living the Word therefore includes advocacy for the voiceless, integrity in leadership, and compassion in community life.

The Spirit keeps justice from turning into self-righteousness. He anchors activism in adoration so that pursuit of fairness flows from fellowship with God. When believers act justly, love mercy, and walk humbly, they display Scripture's moral beauty to a cynical world. The Word lived through justice becomes both protest and prophecy - a glimpse of God's kingdom on earth as it is in heaven.

The Word and perseverance in trials

Living the Word is not tested in comfort but in challenge. Faithfulness shines most brightly when circumstances darken. James wrote, *"Consider it pure joy, my brothers and sisters, whenever you face trials of many kinds, because you know that the testing of your faith produces perseverance."* (James 1:2-3) The Spirit transforms suffering into soil for growth when the believer clings to the promises of Scripture. Every trial invites a choice: to trust feelings or to trust the Word. Feelings fluctuate; the Word endures.

The psalmist confessed, *"My comfort in my suffering is this: Your promise preserves my life."* (Psalm 119:50). When the Word becomes our anchor, storms cannot uproot us. The Spirit reminds us of what God has spoken when everything else seems silent. In pain, the Word proves itself true.

Perseverance is not stoic endurance but Spirit-sustained confidence. The believer who lives the Word in suffering demonstrates that Scripture's promises are not theory but reality. Every tear becomes testimony, every valley becomes validation that God's Word still stands.

"Though the mountains be shaken and the hills be removed, yet my unfailing love for you will not be shaken." (Isaiah 54:10) Living the Word means believing that even when life breaks, God's truth holds.

The Word and the practice of gratitude

Obedience matures into gratitude. The one who lives the Word learns to see grace everywhere. *"Give thanks in all circumstances; for this is God's will for you in Christ Jesus."* (1 Thessalonians 5:18). Gratitude turns the ordinary into worship and suffering into sanctification. It is the posture of a heart saturated with Scripture, aware that every good and perfect gift comes from above.

Gratitude protects against bitterness and pride. The ungrateful heart forgets God's faithfulness; the thankful heart remembers. Israel's wilderness story reminds us how quickly complaint can replace praise. The Spirit teaches us to rehearse God's goodness rather than our grievances. *"Praise the Lord, my soul, and forget not all his benefits."* (Psalm 103:2). Living the Word means keeping gratitude as our default response, even when the reasons are hidden.

A grateful believer becomes a radiant witness. Thankfulness is evangelism in its simplest form - the declaration that God is good. When gratitude governs speech, joy multiplies and anxiety diminishes. The Spirit writes thanksgiving into our reflexes so that worship becomes the language of daily life.

The Word and the fellowship of suffering

To live the Word is to share in the sufferings of Christ. *"For it has been granted to you on behalf of Christ not only to believe in him, but also to suffer for him."* (Philippians 1:29). The Holy Spirit turns persecution and pain into participation in the gospel. When believers endure hardship for righteousness' sake, they display the cross-shaped nature of love.

Suffering shared in Christ's name becomes a sacred fellowship. It refines faith and reveals authenticity. Peter encouraged the church, *"Rejoice inasmuch as you participate in the sufferings of Christ, so that you may be overjoyed when his glory is revealed."* (1 Peter 4:13). Living the Word in adversity testifies that the same Spirit who comforted Jesus in Gethsemane now comforts His followers.

This fellowship of suffering binds believers together across time and culture. The persecuted church in one place strengthens the comfortable church in another. Through their endurance, the global Body learns that Scripture is sufficient even in chains. The Spirit turns pain into proclamation; wounds become witnesses that the Word cannot be imprisoned.

The Word and the hope of renewal

Living the Word is living in anticipation. The promises of Scripture always point forward - to redemption complete and creation restored. *"He who was seated on the throne said, 'I am making everything new!'"* (Revelation 21:5). The Holy Spirit keeps believers hopeful by reminding them that every command obeyed and every burden carried has eternal significance.

The Bible's story ends not with despair but with renewal. The same Word that spoke the universe into being will one day speak the final restoration of all things. Until then, living the Word means walking in hope. *"We wait for the blessed hope – the appearing of the glory of our great God and Saviour, Jesus Christ."* Titus 2:13). The Spirit sustains this expectancy, transforming waiting into worship.

Hope fuels perseverance. When believers live by the promises of God's Word, despair cannot dominate. The Spirit whispers assurance that what is written will be fulfilled, what is begun will be completed, and what is broken will be healed. Living the Word is therefore an act of prophetic faith - declaring by obedience that the kingdom of God is already breaking in.

The Word becomes our life

Ultimately, to live the Word is to live Christ Himself, for He is the Word made flesh. The goal of Scripture is not mastery of a text but maturity in a Person. *"For to me, to live is Christ and to die is gain."* (Philippians 1:21). The Spirit's mission is to reproduce the life of Jesus in every believer until the Bible's message takes human form again.

When Scripture moves from page to practice, God's glory fills ordinary existence. The believer becomes a living translation of divine truth - imperfect yet inspired by grace. The Spirit ensures that the story of redemption continues, not by new revelation but by renewed obedience. *"If anyone obeys his word, love for God is truly made complete in them."* (1 John 2:5)

The life that lives the Word points beyond itself. It becomes a lighthouse of grace in a dark world, drawing others toward the Author of life. The Spirit and the Word together form a melody that will one day crescendo in eternity. Until that final chorus, we are called to keep living the Word - breathing Scripture, walking love, and shining truth - until faith becomes sight and the written Word becomes the living reality of the new creation.

EPILOGUE: THE BIBLE STILL SPEAKS

Not just then, but now

If this book has shown anything, it is this: the Bible is not a museum piece. It is not a relic to be admired behind glass, nor a sacred artefact we dust off on Sundays. It is the living, breathing Word of the living, breathing God. *"The word of God is alive and active."* (Hebrews 4:12). Those words were not written as poetry but as reality. The same Spirit who once spoke through prophets and apostles still speaks through these pages today.

We have traced how Scripture came to be - how God revealed, inspired, and preserved His Word. We have seen how the canon formed, how the Spirit guided the church to recognise what He Himself had breathed out. We have explored why the Bible can be trusted, how context protects us from distortion, and how the Spirit illuminates what He first inspired. But all of that leads to one simple, staggering conclusion: God is still speaking.

He speaks through stories written long ago, now freshly applied. He speaks through promises whispered into new fears, through commands that confront old habits, through warnings that cut through modern lies. The distance between "then" and "now" disappears when the Spirit opens the text. What once sounded like ancient history suddenly sounds like God leaning close and saying, *"This is for you."*

The voice behind the verses

Behind every verse of Scripture stands a Voice. The Bible is not just a book *about* God's words; it *is* God's Word. When we read it, we are not merely handling information; we are being addressed. Jesus said, *"My sheep listen to my voice; I know them, and they follow me."* (John 10:27). That voice is not sentimental imagination - it is the reality of the risen Christ speaking by His Spirit through His Word. This means the goal of Bible reading is not to master a text but to meet a Person. We do not open Scripture simply to accumulate facts but to encounter the God who still speaks through it.

The Spirit takes ink on a page and turns it into a living conversation. A psalm becomes a personal prayer. A gospel scene becomes Christ standing before us again. A letter to a first-century church becomes the Spirit's counsel to our own congregation. The question, then, is not, *Is God speaking?* The question is, *Are we listening?* The tragedy of our time is not that the Bible has grown silent but that our hearts have grown crowded. The Word is clear; our lives are noisy. Yet to every generation, the Spirit extends the same invitation: make room, slow down, open the book - and listen.

The Bible in an age of noise

We live in the noisiest age in human history. Our world hums with constant messages - notifications, podcasts, opinions, headlines. Every screen claims our attention; every voice insists it is urgent. In such a world, the Bible can seem quiet, almost hidden. But its quietness is not weakness; it is wisdom. *"Be still, and know that I am God."* (Psalm 46:10). The Word does not shout over the chaos; it stands above it.

The Bible speaks with a different kind of authority. It does not compete for our amusement; it confronts our allegiances. It does not chase trends or adjust its message to the latest mood. Its truth stands steady while the world constantly rewrites itself. *"The grass withers and the flowers fall, but the word of our God endures forever."* (Isaiah 40:8). Every culture has its own slogans; only Scripture has its promises.

Yet the choice remains ours. We can drift with the noise and let our hearts be shaped by whatever is loudest, or we can anchor ourselves in the Word that outlives every headline. The Bible still speaks - but it will not speak over us. It speaks to those who choose to sit, open its pages, and say, *"Speak, Lord, your servant is listening."*

The Bible in the hands of the church

God did not entrust His Word to isolated individuals; He placed it in the hands of His people. The Bible belongs to the church - not as a possession to control, but as a calling to steward.

"These commandments that I give you today are to be on your hearts. Impress them on your children. Talk about them when you sit at home and when you walk along the road."(Deuteronomy 6:6–7). Long before printing presses, sermons, or study guides, the people of God were called to live this Word together.

The church's health will always mirror its relationship to Scripture. When the Bible is honoured, heard, and obeyed, the church becomes radiant - humble, holy, and hopeful. When the Bible is neglected or twisted, the church loses its voice and its way. Revival has never come from clever strategies; it has always come when the people of God rediscovered the Word of God under the power of the Spirit of God.

In every congregation, in every age, the Spirit asks the same question: will you let the Bible truly shape you? Not just your statements of faith, but your shared life? Not only your sermons, but your relationships, your priorities, your mission? The Bible still speaks - but it speaks loudest through a church that actually lives what it reads.

The Bible in the hands of ordinary believers

One of the great joys of the new covenant is that Scripture is not reserved for scholars and specialists. The Spirit has made the Word accessible to ordinary believers in ordinary places. *"They will all be taught by God."* (John 6:45). That promise is not limited to classrooms or pulpits; it belongs to kitchen tables and quiet lounges, to lunch breaks and late-night prayers. You do not need to be an expert to hear God in Scripture. You need to be available. Yes, there is depth to explore and context to respect. Yes, teachers and resources can serve you well. But the same Spirit who breathed out this Word delights to speak it into the heart of any believer who comes humbly. *"The unfolding of your words gives light; it gives understanding to the simple."* (Psalm 119:130)

The Bible still speaks when a parent reads a single psalm over a sleeping child. It still speaks when a new believer stumbles through the Gospels for the first time, meeting Jesus in every chapter.

It still speaks when a weary saint clings to one promise in the dark and whispers, *"I will trust you."* The power is not in our reading skill but in the Spirit who meets us as we read.

The Bible and the world to come

The Bible not only speaks to us in the present; it also speaks *ahead* of us into eternity. Its story points forward, urging us to look beyond the temporary to the everlasting. *"Heaven and earth will pass away, but my words will never pass away."* (Matthew 24:35). When every empire falls and every ideology fades, the Word of God will still stand. It speaks of what will be when redemption is complete - when Jesus reigns and God's glory fills the earth.

Scripture teaches us to interpret the present through the lens of that promised future. It reminds us that injustice, suffering, and death do not have the final word. God's final Word has already been spoken in Christ, and it echoes through the ages: *"Behold, I am making everything new."* (Revelation 21:5). The Bible still speaks of hope because the Author is not finished with His story. Living in the Word means living in anticipation, carrying the certainty of God's promises into the uncertainty of our days.

The Bible and the presence of the Spirit

How does this Word continue to speak so clearly across millennia? Because the same Spirit who inspired it continues to interpret it. *"But the Advocate, the Holy Spirit, whom the Father will send in my name, will teach you all things and will remind you of everything I have said to you."* (John 14:26) The Spirit is not an external commentator but the internal interpreter of the Bible. He brings the written Word to life in each believer, contextualising ancient truth for modern moments.

When we open the Bible, the Spirit is already there - ready to convict, comfort, and counsel. He whispers truth to the humble and reveals Jesus to the seeker. The Spirit ensures that God's Word never becomes obsolete or irrelevant. In every language and generation, He translates eternal truth into living speech. This is why, across continents and cultures, believers can testify with one voice: *"The Bible still speaks - and it spoke to me today."*

The Bible and the testimony of history

If we listen carefully, we can hear the echoes of this Word through every age of the church. It spoke to Augustine in the garden, to Luther before the Diet of Worms, to Wesley on Aldersgate Street, to countless believers in prisons, pulpits, and mission fields. The Word has outlived its critics, outlasted its suppressors, and outshone its rivals. Empires have fallen trying to silence it, yet it remains. *"The word of the Lord endures forever."* (1 Peter 1:25)

Every revival in history has been born in renewed attention to Scripture. When the Bible is opened, hearts are opened. When it is neglected, the flame dims. The Word has carried the church through reformations, renewals, and revolutions. Its voice still calls nations to repentance and comforts martyrs in the dark. No weapon has ever silenced it because no power can silence God. The Bible's endurance is itself evidence that the Author is alive.

The modern world, for all its noise and knowledge, still needs that ancient voice. Science can describe creation, but only Scripture can reveal its Creator. Philosophy can ask why we exist, but only the Bible shows Who gives that existence meaning. Technology can amplify voices, but only the Bible carries the voice that saves.

The Bible and the purpose of the church

The church's mission is not to invent new truth but to proclaim the old truth freshly. *"Preach the word; be prepared in season and out of season."* (2 Timothy 4:2). Every generation must hear again what God has already said. The Bible still speaks because God's purpose has not changed: to call the lost home, to shape the found into Christ's likeness, and to fill the earth with His glory.

When the church silences the Word, she forfeits her authority. When she speaks the Word in the Spirit's power, the world hears heaven. The Bible still speaks through every faithful sermon, every translated copy, every whispered prayer over an open page.

The Spirit continues to use it as His primary instrument for conviction, conversion, and complete transformation. The Great Commission remains anchored in this conviction: we go with the Word of the living God.

The Bible and the heart of Christ

Above all, the Bible still speaks because Jesus still speaks – as He said in John 6:63, *"The words I have spoken to you – they are full of the Spirit and life."* Every page points to Him; every promise finds its fulfilment in Him. The Bible's authority, beauty, and power all flow from its central figure: the living Word, Jesus Christ, who became flesh and dwelt among us. To read Scripture rightly is to hear the heartbeat of Christ.

The journey of this book began with revelation and ends with relationship. God has not stopped revealing Himself, but the revelation now has a face, a voice, and a name. *"The Word became flesh and made his dwelling among us."* (John 1:14). And through the Scriptures, that same Word still dwells among us today.

The final word

The Bible still speaks because the Author still lives. He has not run out of words or wonders. Every time His people open the Book in faith, heaven bends low to listen and to speak again. The world may change, but the voice of God will never grow silent. It still calls sinners to grace, disciples to obedience, and the church to faithfulness.

The final challenge is not to defend the Bible's relevance but to demonstrate it. When believers live the Word, they prove that it still speaks. When congregations embody its truth in love, the Word becomes visible once more. When the Spirit animates that obedience, the Bible then sings across all the centuries with undiminished power.

So let the final line echo the first truth: *The Bible still speaks.* And if we will listen - and live - it will speak through us.

.

www.ingramcontent.com/pod-product-compliance
Lightning Source LLC
Chambersburg PA
CBHW051731020426
42333CB00014B/1257